A GUI[image] to

D0512835

B EHAVIORAL ECONOMICS

Hugh Schwartz

Printed in the United States of America

Higher Education Publications, Inc., Falls Church, Virginia

ISBN-13: 978-0-914927-61-7
ISBN-10: 0-914927-61-2

Library of Congress Control Number: 2008941525

Contents

Preface

This short book attempts to provide a substantive introduction to behavioral economics for a general audience, and for introductory and intermediate level students of the social sciences, business administration and law. A select bibliography is divided into introductory, intermediate level and more advanced level offerings.

The presentation is an updated version of *Rationality Gone Awry: Decision Making Inconsistent with Economic and Financial Theory* (Westport, CT, and London, 1998, Praeger, paperback, 2000.) Research in behavioral economics has exploded since then, but while surveying the extraordinary amount of new material, *A Guide to Behavioral Economics* is more concise, aimed at encouraging the general reader to take a closer look at the field, and at helping to orient students who are being exposed to so much in so many disciplines. The main effort here is to offer a relatively complete overview and, at the same time, to raise some important questions and point to a few major thrusts that many leading behavioral economists are not giving much attention in their writngs for the general public. Preliminary presentations of parts of this *Guide* were published in *Business Economics*, the magazine of the National Association of Business Economics, and in Morris Altman´s *Handbook of Contemporary Behavioral Economics*. Fuller versions were given in courses in the School of Social Sciences of the University of the Republic (Uruguay) and at the 25th annual conference of the Society for the Advancement of Behavioral Economics (SABE) at New York University.

Reader reactions would be most appreciated.

I am grateful to Donald Hester for comments to the first third of what follows and to Ken Jacobson for the observations throughout, of a journalist who read the piece with the general reader in mind.

1

Introduction

The Economist, the New York Times Magazine and other periodicals have increased their number of articles about behavioral economics in recent years, but most readers of those publications probably wonder why it is being singled out for any special attention. Not that the exposition of economists has always been so clear, but hasn't economics always attempted to deal with economic behavior?

Certainly it is supposed to have done so, but, in reality, we are just beginning to understand some of the limitations of the economic analysis we have been relying on. Behavioral economics represents an effort to improve the ability of economics to deal with actual economic life, and an increasing number of prominent economists have begun to incorporate the findings of behavioral economics into their analytical structure. Behavioral economics builds on existing foundations of mainstream economics, differing from more dissident approaches that would simply deny the validity of much of that analysis of economic phenomena. As more economists come to accept and incorporate more of these new findings, the approach is likely to become such an integral part of the toolkit of economic analysis that we will no longer refer to a distinct "behavioral economics." Several introductions to behavioral economics and behavioral finance have been published recently but most are aimed at professional economists and advanced students of the subject. One of several publications that aims at a broader audience is Dan Ariely's *Predictably Irrational*. While it provides a fascinating overview of behavioral economics experiments, particularly those of Ariely and his collaborators, the book deals almost exclusively with consumer behavior, and even at that, seems to accept the results of the experiments as indicative of what happens in the real world, ignoring any tendency of consumers (not to mention businessmen and investors) to learn from experience.

At the end of these pages I suggest the types of behavioral as well as traditional considerations that might be taken into account in evaluating

1

what to do about two of the country's most pressing long term issues, global warming and health insurance (and I take note of Richard Thaler and Cass Sunstein's recent book, *Nudge*, read subsequently, which is much more ambitious in its proposed applications). To begin, though, consider two easier categories of decisions.

The initial group:

A businessman, on a trip to a city to which he is unlikely to return, has lunch along the way and leaves a tip—even though he doesn't have to, is not doing so to assure good service for any future meal there, and may himself be experiencing difficult times. An individual is offered $200 without having to do anything, as his share of the $1000 a friend has been given to divide between the two—and he rejects the prospective windfall as an unfair (inadequate) division of the gains (at least in laboratory trials). A business economist who claims that optimization based on careful calculation underlies his company's success, draws up a ten-year projection of costs in which possibly dominating productivity growth is estimated by a rule of thumb obtained by averaging what took place in a what he feels is a representative three-year period in the past. An industrial economist sees his company mistakenly undertaking the same pricing policy as the much larger industry leader, but holds back in expressing his disagreement at a Board of Directors meeting because the CEO has just voiced his strong endorsement of that pattern. A nation enraged by TV reports of children sickened by industrial pollution near a housing development, approves legislation intent on eliminating the possibility that such a phenomenon can occur again, even as analyses emerge questioning the magnitude of the damage done, and as the cost of the new regulations comes to greatly exceed what was anticipated.

Now consider another group of decisions.

An investor, finally recognizing that a stock he purchased is most unlikely to outperform the market, decides to sell it—but only after the stock regains the price that he paid for it. Government ministers in charge of a supersonic jet project that will cut travel time across the Atlantic by half, but is incurring costs billions of dollars more than anticipated, decide to push ahead with the task primarily because so much money already has been spent on it. More than half of those residing in flood-prone areas decline heavily subsidized government insurance against flooding. Experienced physicians presented with symptoms of a serious disease and indications of the percentage of those afflicted who are expected to die, recommend a course of medical treatment differing from that suggested by equally experienced specialists who are told of the same symptoms but with the prognosis presented in terms of the percentage of those expected to *survive*.

Such decisions take place often in everyday life, but they are inconsistent with the assumptions about economic behavior that characterize the theory underlying mainstream economics. Of those in the first group, the first three represent decision making that is rational, taking account of a range of considerations that the society regards as just or that reflect a short cut approximation where careful and complete calculation is not feasible. The fourth flaunts rationality in the traditional sense but may be understandable if the economist believes that a candid evaluation would undermine his influence on other subjects that are equally or more important to the company, or, perhaps, simply, if doing so would cost him his job. The fifth reveals the role of emotions in triggering us to make careful calculations but also reflects the fact that emotions can lead to a failure to take costly overreaction into account. On the other hand, the four types of decisions in the second paragraph are simply irrational in economic terms, reflecting psychological tendencies that many of us have, but that have no meaningful cultural justification or saving grace.

Mainstream economics has made major advances in explaining human behavior—extending beyond the field of economics itself, indeed, even to such matters as love and marriage. Incentives can certainly matter, as the recent best selling and essentially mainstream analysis, *Freakonomics* makes clear, and Robert Frank's recent book, *The Economic Naturalist: In Search of Explanations for Everyday Enigmas* shows just how far basic economic principles can take us (and where it is necessary to call on something more). The assumptions of mainstream economics have kept the analyses manageable and most seem to make sense for the long run. It has become increasingly apparent that the assumptions of traditional economic models are not satisfactory to deal with some situations, however, and that reveals itself in some of the examples of Frank and his students. A more behavioral approach is called for. Work on "micro motives" such as that outlined by recent Nobel Prize winner, Thomas Schelling provided an important step in this process, as did the even earlier evidence presented by Herbert Simon and his colleagues showing that we are limited in the extent to which we can be completely rational in our calculations.

Mainstream economic analysis begins by assuming that individuals and their organizations attempt to do the best possible—and that the goal of optimization is feasible, that those who succeed do so because they come closest to doing the best that is possible. Mainstream economic analysis assumes that people consider only their own personal welfare, that they are reasonably well-informed and that they attempt to fill key informational gaps (even when time pressures prevail). Mainstream theory assumes that people possess sufficient reasoning ability to solve simple problems in the best way possible and that they seek appropriate help in solving more complex ones when the benefits for doing so appear to be larger than the costs (and that in those cases that they understand the reasoning of any outside experts they call upon). Another key assumption is that the more the competitive market pressures—the more there are others who are trying to sell the same product or provide the same service—the more likely it is that those who survive will be the ones who have been most nearly able to optimize; the market will see to that, even if individuals themselves are not entirely capable or if they do not exert themselves as much as they might all of the time.

Rigorous analysis that begins with such simplifying assumptions often provides useful guidelines for understanding what takes place (remarkably). Yet all too often, economic forecasts deal with matters that extend beyond the reach of any theoretical base and prove mistaken. This was true, for example, of the Gross Domestic Product projections of the Kennedy Administration, which were prepared by several of the country's most outstanding academics. Perhaps more significantly, some economic analyses of the past need to be substantially revised. Even Nobel Prize winners in economics and finance find that seemingly rational processes of investing sometimes yield results that turn out to be mistaken, as some market participants violate behavioral patterns that would seem to be in their interest and as sufficient arbitrage fails to materialize (or remain in effect).[1]

[1] Arbitrage refers to the simultaneous purchase and sale of the same or very similar securities, commodities or foreign exchange in different markets to profit from dissimilar prices in two or more markets.

Recall the collapse of Long Term Capital Management in the late 1990s and the serious difficulties of several prominent investment banks and hedge funds since that time.

Evaluating economic behavior without taking account of the findings of psychology is like dealing with quantitative relationships without using readily available techniques of mathematics. Nonetheless, since the beginning of the twentieth century, mainstream economics has done just that, limiting itself to the assumption of optimization or to others incorporated on an ad hoc basis that have struck individual economists as plausible for the time and circumstances. But investors often continue to hold onto stocks that have declined in value and have poorer prospects than other options available to them. American industries that export most successfully are not those highly competitive branches with many rivals such as clothing and woodworking, and public television has raised most of its funds from voluntary contributions despite seemingly persuasive theoretical arguments about freeloading.

Behavioral economics rests on assumptions about human behavior that reflect the results of psychological studies, and, as they become firmly established, the findings of the other social sciences and biology. It endeavors to provide descriptively accurate assumptions about the cognitive abilities and emotional responses of humans in their economic decision making, taking account both of institutions—organizational arrangements and the norms of social interaction—and, importantly, of context, of specific circumstances. It allows for variability of effort in response to emotional states as well as incentives. Some of the assumptions coincide with those of mainstream economics, but others do not, or they do not in some contexts. A behavioral approach to economics is essential, not only because the traditional normative model is not entirely realistic—no model ever is—but because the mainstream model does not predict well enough and because its predictions have not been improving much despite major advances in the availability of data, the creation of programs to deal with data, and in the sophistication of measurement techniques.

Traditional economic analysis focuses on how to allocate resources efficiently. That is supposed to maximize welfare for consumers (or offer the potential of achieving that), enabling consumers to do the best that is possible. Behavioral economics indicates that there are serious limits to that theory insofar as it describes how humans actually behave. To the extent that behavioral economics has come to provide normative guidelines, it focuses more modestly on how to move economic behavior away from manifestly poor choices towards better ones—without venturing whether the result comes particularly close to any standard of optimization, which it contends, often is simply not ascertainable, in any event. It is concerned not only with what takes place when supply and demand are neatly in balance, but when, as is so often the case, market forces are in disequilibrium, as is common after shocks to the system such as natural catastrophes, outbreaks of war, unanticipated bankruptcies and other market failures often due to a lack of information or to an incorrect perception of it, and, of increasing importance, because of breakthrough technological innovations.

Behavioral economics considers whether there are *regularities* in what have been termed *anomalies*—the inconsistencies of what happens in actual life with mainstream economic theory—whether what that theory indicates should happen if we succeed in doing the best possible, fails to occur on a predictable basis. Behavioral economics endeavors to provide an approach for dealing with economic behavior in the real world, i.e., it endeavors to provide approaches for dealing with economic problems when optimization is not feasible or the cost of obtaining, what in theory, would be the best solution, would exceed the benefits obtained. It might be advisable to abandon a project after it has been shown to have serious deficiencies, as economic analysis would advocate, but are there alternatives that merely avoid those that are among the worst for dealing with the situation when it seems difficult to abandon altogether, once-favored undertakings and those who have become involved in them? Even more important, perhaps, when *risk averters* find themselves inadvertently becoming *risk takers* because they are so concerned with the emerging prospects of losing (betting on smaller likelihoods than before, trying to recover much of a day's losses in the last race scheduled), are there ways to reduce if not eliminate this tendency so counter to their basic intentions and prospects?

Most behavioral economics has been micro in focus, but some also deals with macroeconomic analysis, most notably with the micro foundations of macro analysis. To the extent that the findings of behavioral economics are incorporated into economic theory, the latter shifts from a purely deductive theory, as has been the case to date, to an increasingly inductive one, relying on empirical findings, much as biology does. The principal standard by which behavioral economics should be judged is whether the more complex approach predicts sufficiently better to justify its additional cost, or, in those cases in which the approach of behavioral economics is less complex, in which the lesser cost is great enough to warrant sacrifice of the benefits forgone by feasible optimization.

The findings of behavioral economics appear to offer hope for improving our ability to deal more effectively than formerly, with such complex interdisciplinary matters as health, environmental safety, organizational behavior and national development. That is, in addition to providing more accurate description and prediction, behavioral economics offers a normative potential, contributing to public policy decision making and economic welfare—though as observed during the current financial crisis and economic slowdown (2007-2008), not yet nearly as much in macroeconomic matters as would be desirable.

2

The Background

By the beginning of the twentieth century, mainstream economic analysis ignored other disciplines, for the most part. It had not always been that way, however. Adam Smith, the first modern economist, also anticipated important findings of the late twentieth century psychologists two decades before writing *The Wealth of Nations* in *The Theory of Moral Sentiments*. Two generations after Smith, another prominent theorist wrestled with psychological considerations, and in the middle of the nineteenth century, John Stuart Mill incorporated conclusions of a political and sociological nature in his work, anticipating the recent concerns of many behavioral economists with the relevance of social and ethical factors to economic behavior. Afterwards, several eminent economic theorists adopted results of the newly emerging field of psychology that were consistent with the assumption of economists that individuals were rational and sought to optimize.

Following that, in the early 20th Century, Vilfredo Pareto provided the foundations of welfare economics, but then turned increasingly to sociology. Alfred Marshall's late 19th-early 20th Century treatises seemed to invite the incorporation of findings from the other social sciences, but the tendency to take note of the work of psychologists waned as the studies of the latter began to cast doubt on some of their own earlier conclusions and as the work of Leon Walras gave further impetus to the use of mathematics to calculate conditions of what was deemed economic optimality. In 1918, J. M. Clark lamented that economics could not ignore psychology—the evolving findings of psychology—it was only a matter of whether economics used good psychology or bad.

Clark's remarks went unheeded, however. Even the psychological speculations of the most prominent American economist of the first half of the 20th Century, Irving Fisher about the motivations underlying intertemporal decisions could not turn the tide; his own, much earlier writings calling for the independence of economics, and the similar views of most other major economists, held sway. Avoidance of the other social sciences became even more pronounced by the late 1930s and in the period after the Second World War (despite some intriguing psychological dicta by John Maynard Keynes, the father of modern macroeconomics and a most successful investor). It was not that most mainstream economists believed that the assumptions they used reflected human behavior accurately. Rather, as Milton Friedman contended in 1953, they believed the adequacy of economic theory should be judged by its ability to predict; successful economic agents tended to behave as *if* they took account of all of the factors that economists considered relevant, whether or not those agents were conscious of that behavior, it was contended. The oft-repeated example: the successful billiards player who was unaware of the relevant laws of physics and mathematics.

There were exceptions throughout the years, but they were not influential. Institutional economists of the late 19th and early 20th Centuries, led by the German Historical School and J.R. Commons, rejected most mainstream analysis. Veblen, a member of that group, wrote insightfully about "conspicuous consumption" and preferences that were dependent on persons other than an individual him- or herself. He was regarded as an outsider, however, and the appreciation of what he had done improved only slightly with the related work of Duesenberry and Leibenstein during the late 1940s and early 1950s. At the close of the Second World War, psychologist Katona so doubted the conclusions of most macro analysts projecting a forthcoming recession that he set about surveying what consumers and producers actually felt, what their expectations were and what they planned to do. Those efforts proved so useful that were quickly adopted as a new standard practice by the economics profession for macroeconomic projections—but Katona never expounded an alternative theory of economic behavior. Later, economists such as Marschak, Radner and Markowitz provided important qualifications to an uncritical application of the dominant approach to microeconomic analysis (some of which anticipated the positions of subsequent key figures in behavioral economics), but they are best remembered for their contributions to mainstream analysis. Nonetheless, at the same time that Friedman was laying down the dicta noted above, subsequent Nobel Prize laureate, Simon and his colleagues at the management faculty of the then Carnegie Institute of Technology went about interviewing business enterprises and presented analyses on *bounded* rationality that provided the underlying support for behavioral economic analysis.

3

Bounded Rationality

In its basic form, mainstream economic theory assumes that rationality is complete—that humans are capable of reasoning fully what is in their economic interest—the survivors in any event—and that this is reinforced by the competition of the marketplace. It is assumed that we possess all the necessary information or undertake rational efforts to obtain it. Initially, at least, it was assumed that there is a relatively costless process of decision making as to how to optimize productive efficiency and consumer welfare as well as investment.

Simon and his colleagues dissented from the prevailing view of economic rationality, and pointed to "slack" in the way in which even resources which are efficiently allocated to the various industries and services, are actually employed (a lack of x-efficiency, in the terminology of Leibenstein). Economic agents lack the data, the programs to handle the data, and the cognitive ability to optimize, it was maintained. They are engaged in bounded (limited) rationality, and seek to "satisfice" rather than to maximize. Instead of attempting to earn the highest level of profits possible, they may seek only to do better than before or better than their competitors. Simon conjectured that they seek to reach some level of aspirations (which may vary according to their success in achieving aspirations levels in the past). The lack of x-efficiency has been verified in many studies and though acknowledged (in passing) in many economics texts, there has been little effort to introduce this common phenomenon into the analysis; the graphs and equations of mainstream analysis have remained unchanged.

The concept of bounded rationality was introduced into mainstream analysis, but as maximization that is constrained, and that is dealt with in a traditional rational manner rather than as the Black Box that it is. Moreover, as scarce as some information often is, Simon held that the scarcest resource of all may be attention, related to which is the fact that signals are not perceived equally by all persons. The first important aspect, differences in the information often in the hands of buyers and sellers (the asymmetry of information) was underscored in a path-braking article by Akerlof on the market for used cars, and the role of asymmetrical information gained further importance with the contributions of Stiglitz and his collaborators. Some individuals maintain that the existence of transaction costs—expenses such as those incurred in monitoring employee behavior and enforcing contracts and other legal rights with those outside a firm, explains why rationality is necessarily bounded, and most who work on transaction costs analysis believe that mainstream analysis can accommodate such matters.

Simon and his followers maintained that bounded rationality entailed *procedural* rationality, which contrasted with the rationality of mainstream economics, an ex post phenomenon which they characterized as *substantive* rationality. Later, influenced by population biologists, Simon and others questioned whether survival rather than maximization was not the most rational objective, noting that survival could call for procedures different from those of maximization (since the latter might include taking on situations that could lead to a failure to survive). While it can make sense in terms of mainstream economic reasoning to put off making a choice until a larger number of alternatives becomes available, behavioral economics helps explain the frequently observed difficulty of making a selection in the presence of a particularly large number of alternatives.

Simon's contention that decision makers deal with bounded rationality by "satisficing" was rejected by most economists as too vague to be helpful—though Selten, who was to win a Nobel Prize for work of a more traditional nature, built on Simon's explanation of satisficing in terms of achieving a level of aspirations. This was developed more fully when he became part of the small, but increasing number of prominent theorists (beginning with Arrow in 1982) who have contributed to a manifestly behavioral approach. In 1996 Conlisk summarized the evidence on bounded rationality, which has been increasingly taken into account in the applied economic analyses even of many mainstream economists. Moreover, as several of the writings of Simon imply and other economists later stated more explicitly, human beings do not always perceive information accurately, further complicating the issue of economic rationality; people often address themselves to problems that are variants of the ones they actually confront. Beyond that, while mainstream economics assumes that people perceive and act upon marginal differences, the evidence shows that sometimes we perceive, and often, we act upon differences only when they are more than marginal—when they constitute a Just Noticeable Difference, to use the terminology of a few writers.

Finally, it is necessary to take account of the fact that the response of individuals to what they feel that they gain with additions to income, and what they endure with additions to risk (and uncertainty), tend to vary with the levels of income, risk and uncertainty (along with many aspects of context); it is necessary to take the diminishing marginal utility of income and the often varying sensitivity to risk and uncertainty into account as well as the eventually diminishing marginal productivity of effort. Mainstream economists would not disagree, but this has particular importance for some of the discussions that follow.

The overriding theme of mainstream microeconomic analysis is efficiency in the allocation of resources, and the emphasis is on providing guidelines for achieving that efficiency. Little consideration is given to the cases in which inefficiency is not eliminated, or in which there are long delays in doing so, or to the costs of either. Nor has there been much consideration of the degree to which a better understanding of the full nature of human behavior would either prepare us to expect economic inefficiency in certain contexts and help us reduce those inefficiencies, or to reconsider whether some of what seem, at first glance, to be inefficiencies, might not be rational in some broader sense. Little of a helpful nature has been offered to orient innovation; available cost-benefit analysis provides no really useful guidelines for projects involving technological development (despite work on the subject by eminent economists). Unfortunately, behavioral economics has not yet offered much to alleviate this problem. Bounded rationality remains very much with us.

4

Prospect Theory and other major contributions from psychology

Psychologists had been publishing findings critical of the assumptions of mainstream economic theory for more than a decade, particularly economic psychologists in Europe, but the most dramatic breakthrough for behavioral economics came in the 1970s with the work of cognitive psychologists known as behavioral decision theorists. In the beginning of that decade, Slovic, Lichtenstein and colleagues published studies showing that individuals may change their preferences in the short run, in apparent violation of the transitive reasoning assumption so critical to mainstream economic theory. (Transitive reasoning means that a preference for one item over a second and the second over a third implies a logical preference for the first with respect to the third). At the same time, Kahneman and Tversky were writing about heuristics, simple but often relatively efficient mechanisms for making judgments, and of the biases associated with those short cut substitutes. The articles appeared first in psychology journals, and in 1974, a summary, which suggested that decision makers ordinarily did not use maximizing techniques, appeared in the influential journal, *Science*. At the end of the decade, Kahneman and Tversky published a landmark article in the prominent economics journal, *Econometrica* entitled, "Prospect Theory. An Analysis of Decisions under Risk." Prospect Theory was the name given by Kahneman and Tversky to the manner that they concluded decision makers actually behaved, and is based on laboratory experiments. It reflects possible outcomes and the probabilities of each, and features the following characteristics:

First, most individuals have positive, but declining marginal utility to additions to income, and prefer outcomes that are certain to those that would offer only the probability of a level of income, even when the latter involve a somewhat higher expected value. Most prefer $3,000 with certainty to $4,000 with a probability of .8 even though the expected value of the latter is greater, at $3,200. Those individuals—most people—are what would ordinarily be termed, risk averters. No inconsistency with economic theory here; economic theory certainly allows for a variety of attitudes toward risk, as long as decision makers are consistent in those attitudes.

Second, when confronted with the possibility of losses, people reveal a greater sensitivity than they do for gains and most individuals show an inclination to *assume* risks, or, as they view it, to avoid losses, which Kahneman and Tversky characterized as loss aversion. Subsequent studies have shown that *loss aversion* is characteristic of numerous human undertakings. It is not uncommon for people to reverse their attitude toward risk according to Prospect Theory, whereas the models of traditional economics assume that the attitudes of individuals toward risk, whether favorable or unfavorable, should remain the same, provided only that the gains and losses are small (and do not have what economists call income and wealth effects). Along similar lines, as other observers have noted, people dislike losing commodities from their consumption bundle much more than gaining other commodities.

Third, individuals tend to make decisions on the basis of the prospects for gain or loss from a given reference point rather than from consideration of their overall wealth or the statistically probable outcome of a large number of similar decisions even when it is clear that many are likely to present themselves.[2] Experiments have shown that when individuals are told that there is a two part sequence to take into account (and, thus, that the effect on their wealth can be determined only after taking both steps into account), they, nonetheless, tend to evaluate their gains and losses after each part of the sequence. This makes a difference if a given dollar amount of gains is valued differently than the same amount of losses (and if the amount by which the two differ, varies, as it often does) and if the steps to consider involves both gains and losses. In other words, individuals often make erroneously myopic decisions, considering separately, each of the components that are part of the same package. The same criticism of a mistakenly myopic approach holds in the case of decision situations in which there is only a single component, but when a large number of similar decision situations can be anticipated.

---

[2] Many factors influence the specific reference points, an important matter which behavioral economists have not yet adequately sorted out.

Fourth, the *framing* of the information—the way in which information is presented—is critical; the same information can lead to different decisions, depending on the way in which it is framed, even if it is transparent that the information is identical. Framing can even determine whether some outcomes are viewed as gains or losses and thus whether the outcomes promote risk aversion or risk taking. An extreme example of a framing problem already has been noted: the same data can be characterized as one of 80 per cent positive or 20 per cent negative, and that can lead to differences in the reasoning even of professionals, as was the case in an experiment involving medical specialists. Studies following the Kahneman and Tversky's 1979 article were important in clarifying the significance of framing. Unfortunately, we are not able to estimate the magnitude of differences that can be anticipated from differences in framing, which may vary with context and with the emotional state of those involved.

Fifth, individuals have difficulty in assessing probabilities, particularly small probabilities, which they sometimes overestimate but simply ignore at other times.

The work on prospect theory was cited extensively and led to a Nobel Prize in economics for psychologist Kahneman. Prospect theory may not yet have become a full-fledged component of mainstream analysis, but it is a concept that all economists need to take into account.

Kahneman and Tversky maintained that decision makers continue to act as prospect theory suggests, even given financial incentives to behave in what might be deemed a more optimal manner—in a manner more consistent with the greatest expected value or the greatest expected subjective utility. Prospect theory does not really deal with choices for gains in the small number of situations in which preferences are risk neutral or risk taking. That would seem to be the case, for example, for entrepreneurs, who are largely absent from among the participants in economics and psychology laboratories that have found the phenomenon (and to the extent that they are present, are not considered independently). It is possible, of course, that the different response of entrepreneurs reflects greater self confidence as much as greater risk taking. To the extent that is true, the greater self-confidence may reflect specialized knowledge and/ or managerial capacity (as the capacity of implementing decisions). On the other hand, the greater self-confidence may not be entirely rational. An inclination for relatively risk seeking behavior also seems to be associated with small, low probability gambles, and while this interest in participating in lotteries has been noted by various observers over the years, it would seem to have been of less significance for the economy—though the amounts spent in casinos in recent years may imply that this is changing. In any event, empirical studies have shown that for most people, risk taking/loss averse inclinations are finally reversed when bankruptcy or major adversity seem to be serious possibilities, or even if there is merely some chance of their occurring, when the consequences are viewed as particularly bad (about which, more later).

The contributions of psychology to the assumptions about the attitudes of individuals toward risk and any tendency for them to behave consistently have been verified empirically and have altered descriptive economics profoundly.

5

Preferences, Choice and Utility

Preferences constitute the basic, underlying consideration in explaining choice. Heuristics, short cuts in lieu of complete calculation, also must be taken into account in determining how preferences are translated into choice (see Section 7), as well, in most cases, as strategic interaction with others. Traditional economics has given a great deal of attention to one form of strategic interaction—a mathematical construct known as game theory, and some behavioral economists have focused on a modified version of that—behavioral game theory. More heuristic approaches probably are the dominant approaches to strategic interaction, however, and need to be taken into account though they still have not been much investigated by economists. All three—preferences, heuristics and the result of the various approaches to strategic interaction—contribute to and underlie what we have in mind when we speak of utility. Utility, in turn, can refer to the utility that has been experienced or that which is anticipated. Anticipated utility, the critical factor in decision making, usually is influenced by what has been experienced, of course, though anticipations (expectations) also are influenced by the existing, possibly altered context, and the expected, probably differing context. Finally, the utility that has been experienced ordinarily is recalled imperfectly, and even when remembered accurately, experiments show that we tend to overweight certain moments of the past, most notably the endpoints, rather than taking the total experience into account in a balanced manner. Thus, there may be quite a leap between underlying preferences and the relevant utility—but let's begin with preferences.

The emphasis on preferences (revealed preferences, increasingly) has coincided with avoidance, until recently, of any consideration not only of context, but also of underlying motives and mental states. Yet the latter can be important in assessing preferences and the resulting utility. (See Sections 10 and 12.) The assessment of even the first step in explaining utility, that following from preferences, is particularly difficult inasmuch as choices often involve complex baskets of preferences. Evaluations in terms of utility are further complicated by the growing awareness that the act of consumption may involve costs, especially over time, and that some forms of payment for consumption lead to more discomfort than others. While mainstream economics now allows for the potential of shifts in preferences over time more than it did formerly, due especially to repeated exposure and learning, in most economic models, preferences are generally assumed to be relatively stable at any given point in time.

Mainstream economics assumes that choices reflect relative prices and preferences, given the budget constraint, and that preferences are consistent at any point in time—that they are transitive. Nonetheless, in an experiment more than three decades ago, Slovic and Lichtenstein undermined this basic assumption. In their experiment, participants were asked to choose between two outcomes, one, a *low probability* of a obtaining a large sum of money, and the other, a *high probability* of obtaining a smaller sum of money. The expected value of each was approximately the same. The participants were then given the opportunity to place a *price* on both the low and high probability options and to sell them. Many of those who said that they preferred the first option, assigned a higher price to the second, and vice versa for many of those who stated that they preferred the second option. The surprising results were substantiated later in an experiment in a casino.

This "preference reversal" was challenged by several prominent economists—who, to their surprise, found that most participants in their experiments also revealed reversals of preferences. The psychologists attributed preference reversal to the fact that different heuristics (calculation short cuts) were used in the two cases and that the two are likely to have different biases. Initially, in asking for a choice, the experimenters' use of the word "probability" led participants to respond in terms of a different heuristic than that triggered by use of the word "price," the term used in referring the sale of the options for the two choices. Beyond that, it has come to be recognized that differences in choices in a given moment of time can reflect the fact that preferences, reflecting valuations, are influenced by institutions, context, moods, stress, decision fatigue and other emotional states; also, by prolonged exposure, particularly to tempting stimuli (in part because those factors may influence risk, or the risk that is perceived, and any changes in expectations that all these may engender).

The findings on preference reversal set off a debate concerning the validity of the key assumption that traditional economic models make—the assumption of transitivity—and this raises serious questions about economic welfare. Findings of "inconsistent" preferences have led to a re-examination of some of the basic assumptions about preferences. "Casual" empiricism, reinforced by laboratory experiments, underscore the fact that some choices are made between alternatives, one or more of which are relatively unknown, and for which preferences really have not yet been formed. Moreover, preferences involving hypothetical options or those that do not yet exist may not reflect the values that would be relevant for the phenomena were they to come into being, in part because contexts that might prove to be relevant may not yet exist. Also, the answers that people give when there is not something at stake may not be the same as those given when there is. Individuals may not be able to assess their preferences accurately in situations of the former type. Some preferences are the result of what is experienced *after* choices are made—i.e., they may be malleable, even in the short run. This work on the "construction of preferences" is sometimes cited by behavioral economists, but not yet truly taken into account; laboratory and field experiments seldom consider that some of the preferences in choices being evaluated first evolve during the course of or after the process of selection. The experiments economists have undertaken to date have avoided consideration of choices between options, one or more of which are not known to participants, though the latter certainly occur in real life. They are particularly important in situations in which expectations differ from the reality of the point in time at which decisions are being made (and both the informational base underlying the change in expectations and any biases involved in those expectations also may differ, as Tobias Rötheli has maintained).

Beyond that, there has long been a debate as to how to deal with the conflicting preferences revealed by what some economists have termed "multiple selves." One "self" is said to dominate when it comes to the general case for evaluating the case for saving more—but another takes over when it actually comes to the moment of spending, for example. Thaler has written of the farsighted Planner and the myopic Doer. Similarly, one "self" is assumed to determine the case for consuming or abstaining from consuming drugs in the abstract, but another self takes over when the drugs are presented. It has never been made clear, what triggers the shift from one self to the other. Nonetheless, several economists have extended that approach and argued in favor of "meta" preferences involving what have been characterized as first and second order preferences (to deal with choices for especially hedonistic and/or environmentally damaging alternatives when others regarded as morally, ethically or aesthetically preferable are available, for example).

The strength of something akin to the multiple selves and meta preferences phenomena can be observed in the willingness of people to indicate how they want their own options to be limited in certain circumstances, and to have others (even governments) determine how their options will be limited. We agree to have our hands tied in advance when we accept the obligatory payments of many savings schemes, though more so with certain plans than others, and this is truer for some individuals than others. In the *Odyssey*, Ulysses went quite far, indeed, having the crew tie him to the mast and blindfold him when his ship sailed by the sirens he felt he should resist but which he believed, that left alone, he would not be able to. Beyond this, the traditional view of preferences dealt with those of the individual, with some tendency to consider the preferences of the family, whereas behavioral economics also takes account of "other-regarding" preferences, those that take into account, members of society who are not in the family—for which, see also the discussion of Section 10.

What is involved in the term "preferences," is sometimes much more complicated than traditional economics has been inclined to recognize, and this influences the resulting analysis. Behavioral economics can help distinguish between such situations and those in which preferences are essentially as mainstream economics assumes and it is possible to continue to rely on the analysis already available to us.

6

Anomalies—Inconsistencies with Mainstream Economic Theory

Preference reversal and the apparent violation of logically consistent choice (i.e., of what economists refer to as transitivity) was characterized as an anomaly—a finding inconsistent with microeconomic theory. Ad hoc observations have been reinforced by numerous laboratory experiments and other empirical analyses revealing an extraordinary catalogue of anomalies. Most of the anomalies are predominantly short or intermediate term phenomena, but some prevail over the long run. The anomalies can be catalogued as violations to what Richard Thaler characterized in 1987, as fifteen principles of the rationality of mainstream economics:

1. Cancellation: the choice between two options depends only on the difference between the options, and when one option is preferred to another, the same preference will hold if an identical amount is added to both or subtracted from both (as in algebra).

2. Expectation: the utility of an outcome is weighted by its probability, and if uncertainty is involved in two equivalent alternatives, the origin of the uncertainty should not influence decision choices.

3. Risk Aversion: the utility function for wealth is concave and risk averse, there is a diminishing marginal utility of wealth.

4. Asset integration: an individual's utility is determined by his or her wealth at the final stages of a transaction or set of interrelated transactions, not by adding up the utility at intermediate stages.

5. Preference Ordering: preferences at any point in time are transitive and independent of the method used to elicit them.

6. Invariance: choices between options are independent of the way in which they are described.

7. Dominance: if one option is better than a second in every respect, it can be said to be preferred to that second option.

8. Opportunity Costs: willingness to pay equals willingness to sell (in the absence of income effects and transaction costs), i. e., opportunity and out-of-pocket costs are equal.

9. Marginal Analysis: choices are made to equate marginal costs and marginal benefits.

10. Sunk Costs: fixed, historical and other sunk costs do not influence decisions.

11. Fungibility: money is the same whatever its source and is spent on its highest valued use.

12. Domain of Utility: the willingness to pay for a good depends only on the characteristics of the good, not on the perceived merits of a deal.

13. Economic Opportunities: all legal economic opportunities for gains will be exploited.

14. Rational Expectations: probabilistic judgments are consistent and unbiased.

15. Bayesian Learning: probabilistic judgments are updated by the appropriate use of established statistical techniques. [3]

To this list perhaps should be added, the rationality of decisions from one period of time to another, which is considered in Section 8. Experiments have been added to ad hoc examples, revealing exceptions to all of these principles of economic rationality, giving rise to the recent explosion of interest in behavioral economics. Many of the exceptions are now well recognized and a number of the most prominent of these are noted in this text (with more comprehensive summaries provided in several of the items listed in the Bibliography).

Just a few examples of the anomalies. One is the often striking difference between the price which individuals are willing to pay for goods and services not ordinarily intended for resale and that which, when they are on the other side of the counter, they insist as the minimum they will accept if they are to part with the items (or service). The findings on this come primarily from the experiments of economics laboratories and are dealt with further in Section 13. Another notable piece of evidence from common observation, noted in the Introduction, is the inclination of individuals to tip, often as much in out-of-the-way restaurants to which they never expect to return as in restaurants to which they return regularly and from which they expect good service. Part of the explanation for this behavior may be attributable to a desire for social approval or to avoid

---

[3] Many economists would characterize some of these as axioms and others as assumptions; both are a part of what economists have in mind when they speak of rationality.

feelings of guilt, and much seems simply to reflect treating others in what is regarded as a just manner (see the discussion in Section 12). Yet another anomaly worth noting at the outset is the difference in response sometimes recorded to the identical price according to whether the latter is labeled as a price reduction or a discount; the latter may facilitate acceptance of subsequent increases in price.

Unfortunately, there has not been much effort to indicate the relative frequency with which the tenets of economic rationality are violated, the difficulty of overcoming the anomalies, their cost, nor most of the contexts in which the anomalies are frequent, difficult to overcome and/or costly. There is evidence that the manner of presentation (framing) can play a role in several of these. As an example, information given in terms of frequencies often leads to fewer anomalies than the same information given in terms of probabilities. Similarly, the manner of presentation also influences the degree to which individual reasoning conforms to (or approaches) established statistical techniques. The only major evidence on the frequency of anomalies has come from laboratory tests involving precise repetition of the options, in which case the anomalies have been reduced and sometimes eliminated after several trials. Unfortunately, there is only very limited indication whether (or to what degree) the same holds for repetitions in which there are variations in context, as in real life. This is particularly important because many of the important real life situations are relatively unique, with little opportunity for learning from the type of precise repetition that characterizes the laboratory experiments. Most laboratory experiments have been made with first and second year college students, not businesspersons, investors or actual consumers. The studies assume that teenagers are as likely as older adults with more life experiences to respond rationally —to *all* types of decisions—which is counter to what studies of psychologists and sociologists indicate about the reasoning inclinations of teenagers and those in their early 20s, at least for decisions with a major social content (see, e. g., the Ekert-Jaffe and Grossbard reference). Moreover, no efforts have been made to determine if the individuals in the experiments, whether business persons or even students, make the same decisions in real life contexts as they do in laboratories (which, admittedly, would be much more difficult to assess). Two recent experiments suggest that that may not always be the case.

In the 1970s Kahneman expressed his doubts about our ability to substantially reduce anomalies and attain solutions that are clearly better in terms of traditional criteria. The evidence reveals a mixed picture. The level of financial incentives has been shown to make a difference in many but not all cases. Market experience eliminates some but not all anomalies and actually creates others. Some anomalies such as money illusion, the failure to properly take inflation into account, continue (even if to a reduced degree) despite publicity over many years and the institution of mechanisms which should have helped to eliminate or substantially reduce most such mistaken judgments. In part, this is due to error, but sometimes it may also reflect the particular definition economics has given to rationality or it may reflect the fact that consideration of changes in nominal rather than real money sometimes serves as a heuristic or calculation short cut which may be quite rational in view of deliberation costs in calculating real changes. However, certain financial anomalies such as the tendency for many investors to sell stock market "winners" too soon and to hold on to "losers" too long, seem very nearly impervious to the advice of financial advisors, and occur for reasons that seem to escape any conventional logic. Moreover, despite what would be a normal expectation that the demand for stock shares would increase when prices decline (following a decline in the volume of activity in the market), and that the demand would decrease when share prices increase (following a boom in market activity), ordinarily, just the reverse occurs for substantial periods of time.

Although some anomalies seem to persist, on-going publicity of and commentary about certain anomalies has reduced the occurrence of others. The Winner's Curse, the tendency of those who triumph in auctions, to pay more than reasonable economic value, first noted by petroleum geologists, is an example of that, along with the reduction of the "January Effect," whereby, for many years, small companies experienced major gains in the New York Stock Exchange in the first month of the year for reasons never well understood. No one seems to be looking into the reasons for these differences in the persistence of anomalies, and while we employ controls to reduce the impact of some tendencies towards "irrational" behavior (as Ulysses did in the Odyssey), some deviations in our reasoning are made, as Robert Frank has so aptly phrased it, "without regret," while others are made "with regret." Among these are decisions about important issues of the day such as the evaluation of ecological alternatives or the implementation of policies based on those evaluations. We lack effective strategies to reduce some anomalies at the personal level and, in some cases, seem to have no alternative other than to turn to a regulatory process to do so. (Note, too, that at the personal level we tend to create separate mental accounts for different activities and even different time periods, and reason consistently—treating money as fungible, for example—only within the context of each mental account. Ordinarily, we do not treat a dollar in a savings account as equal to a dollar in a credit card balance, and we are hesitant to withdraw funds from the former to pay off a credit card balance.) An apparent anomaly perhaps beyond the tenets listed above, is that over the past decade or so, the compensation of CEOs in the United States has risen dramatically in relation to that of the average employee in their companies and in relation to CEOs abroad, despite the relative decline in the standing of many of the companies at home and their profitability and value added relative to foreign competition.

Some deviations from the traditional reasoning of economics are intended, as noted, and reflect emotional factors or social preferences, which are discussed below. Still other factors may explain the majority of anomalies. The first of the latter is the use of heuristics, shortcuts in the reasoning process, that almost invariably lead to results that vary from those that would be produced by a complete and careful calculation. Beyond that, the incidence and seriousness of the anomalies may be explained by overconfidence (sometimes under-confidence), a "status quo effect," loss aversion, a desire to avoid ambiguity, an imperfect understanding of probabilities, the statistically incorrect incorporation of new information, inattention to possibly contradictory information, and the fact that we often make judgments based on imperfect (and, worse, not always relevant) recollection of the utility we experienced in the past, rather than on estimates of anticipated utility. Note, though that anticipated utility involves expectations, changes in which also may affect the likelihood of inconsistent reasoning.

Anomalies to any generalized theoretical model can be expected, of course. Concern arises when the anomalies are as pervasive as seems to be the case for the mainstream models of economics. To the extent that the anomalies are not only pervasive but lead to serious errors in prediction that are not eliminated over time with publicity about them, there is a strong argument for modifying the models, at least for contexts in which those limitations hold. Determination of that is a challenge confronting behavioral economics, one that would seem to precede the construction of any new behavioral theory—though it is the latter that is receiving the main thrust of emphasis at present.

7

Heuristics, Context and Biases

Even for those who seek to attain highly favorable results, there are a number of reasons for using heuristics—short cuts for decision making—instead of more precise, optimizing calculations.

To begin with, decision makers may be unaware of the best way to solve many problems even when there clearly is a best way, and they may not have the resources to get others to help them or sufficient access to credit to achieve the same; in addition, the deliberation costs may be excessive.

Second, it may not be possible to obtain all the information necessary for an optimizing solution, or to do so by the time a decision must be made.

Third, while optimization techniques may be feasible, they may not yet have been devised for some types of problems. In any event, problems with multiple objectives almost never lend themselves to unique, optimal solutions.

Fourth, a decision may be needed before relatively extensive optimization calculations can be completed.

Fifth, the use of rules of thumb may enable a decision maker to keep certain matters secret until it is decided to make the decision or even consideration of the matter known.

Sixth, the problem may not be so much in obtaining the information as in *perceiving* it correctly by the time the decision has to be made.

Seventh, an extraordinarily large amount of information may overwhelm the decision maker, not only because of the lack of (or unfamiliarity with) programs to handle the data, but because of the emotional character of the particular decision (or the decision maker, at least in the context involved), the emotionally charged formulation of some data, or the state of awareness of the decision maker.

Eighth, decision makers who ordinarily make optimization calculations may be induced (even if only temporarily) to stray from that course by "winning formulas" of others that only seem to be more successful approaches, but which are characterized by more than offsetting additional risks and, thus, are not warranted by rational considerations.

Heuristics are used to best advantage when there are clear guidelines for the search for information, for the point at which that search should be limited (a stopping rule), and for making a decision based on the information obtained.

Even if there is only a single objective such as profit maximization, the use of heuristics may be advisable if implementation of that objective presents serious difficulties for any reason (even if only for a limited time). Beyond that, the use of heuristics is appropriate where they approximate rather closely what would result from an optimization calculation—if they are what some researchers have termed, fast and frugal heuristics. The latter refers to situations in which the deliberation costs of undertaking so-called optimization calculations would exceed the benefits obtained in doing so—perhaps because the gains from a more complete analysis would be minor, because the heuristics have been greatly improved over time, or because data acquisition would be particularly expensive (as in many new categories of situations).

None of this is to deny that overly simple or otherwise incorrect heuristics are often used, and heuristics are sometimes used where traditional optimization calculations are both feasible and advantageous.

Most heuristics do not lead to results especially close to those of optimization calculations. They involve what Kahneman and Tversky, and most since, refer to as biases. Those heuristics involve deviations from traditional optimizations, but there is disagreement as to whether the biases are just something one should seek to reduce by emphasizing improvement of the heuristics, or, given the cost of doing so, whether the biases are just something to take into account, reflecting results as good as can be expected in terms of a rationality that is more inclusive than that which economists ordinarily have considered.

Mainstream economics provides a set of tools that are most suitable for dealing with a well defined set of alternatives. Yet, as Nelson and

Winter indicated, exploring a poorly defined choice set such as frequently confronts decision makers, is a vastly different activity than optimizing a clearly enunciated one. Indeed, as Simon observed, the first major challenge may arise in the search for all the feasible alternatives, and even when uncovered, the consequences of some of the options may not always be fully grasped in advance. Moreover, when it comes to decisions based on evolving technologies, heuristics to aid in horizon scanning may be more useful than any calculations, as distinguished economists concede and successful innovators insist.

It is necessary to turn to heuristics (rules of thumb) for many judgments. While most rules of thumb may be specific to circumstances, there are general categories of heuristics, and the explanation of these by Kahneman and Tversky led to major inquiry in this area. The initial focus was on Availability, Anchoring and Adjustment, and Representativeness.

Problems may arise in the acquisition of information, and here, availability, perception, problems related to the frequency of data presentation, the concreteness (and vividness) of information, and even the order in which data are presented, all are considerations. Availability biases may arise because the ease with which specifics can be recalled from memory affects judgments about the relative importance of data, leading to over-estimation of the probability of well-publicized or dramatic events (especially recent ones), and media attention can lead to "availability cascades." A prominent example of the availability bias is the belief of most people that homicides (which are highly publicized) are more common than suicides, although the reverse is true. Availability cascades can lead to costly overreactions, even in confronting serious problems such as the Love Canal pollution and the Alwar insecticide contamination of the 1970s in the U. S. Imperfect perception also can be serious. It is accentuated by differences in educational background, life experiences, basic personality, and context. Even when there is an effort to maximize, it is on the basis of *perceived* data which may result in a maximization of a problem that varies from the one actually confronted.

Biases in processing information may begin with incorrect understanding and incorporation of information about probability and payoffs, including a tendency to overvalue certainty and even the *appearance* of certainty, which has been demonstrated in some two-stage experiments.

Another common occurrence is the tendency to ignore very low probabilities, especially prior to natural disasters, but then, after their occurrence, to treat them as if their probabilities were higher than they actually are, even if only temporarily. Kahneman and Tversky emphasized tendencies to overestimate low probabilities but also noted that they were sometimes ignored—in both cases, reflecting the difficulty in evaluating low probabilities correctly. In addition, errors often arise in applying statistical techniques; there are illusory associations or correlations, a tendency to attribute causality to correlations, inappropriate use of linear extrapolation (and incorrect approaches to estimating nonlinear extrapolation), failure to incorporate new information correctly in estimating probabilities and making judgments, and a tendency to seek feedback that confirms results previously obtained (rather than one that attempts to seek contrary evidence). People reveal difficulty in consistently applying criteria; in some cases at least, models based on the enunciated criteria of experts predict better than do the on-going judgments of those very same experts.

Recent studies have emphasized the role of heuristics (simplifying strategies) in biasing information processing—although, as noted, some heuristics come close to optimization calculations, at least in certain contexts. One line of work on simplifying strategies has emphasized attributes.[4] The work on attributes has involved compensatory or non-compensatory decision rules. The other line of simplifying strategies, which has drawn more attention from economists, has emphasized heuristics such as Availability, Anchoring and Representativeness. The judgmental heuristic, Availability, already noted in considering the access to information, involves the effect on the weight given to information because of the ease of recall. The extraordinarily successful mutual fund manager, Peter Lynch, tended to avoid the stocks that most analysts and managers were celebrating because he concluded that such "availability" increased the likelihood that the shares of those companies were overvalued. Anchoring and adjustment refers to essentially mechanical adjustment from a starting point such as recent data on inflation or economic growth or, as in certain experiments, random data, and even false data deliberately injected by individuals serving as "plants," hired by the organizers of experiments to respond with particularly high or low numbers.

---

[4] Some attributes to which people profess not to assign much importance, or which they may even be unaware of, and which may not seem to be relevant, may, nonetheless, have a significant impact on certain of their choices. This applies to some attitudes as well as to attributes.

Representativeness involves judgments of the likelihood of an event or an identification based on its similarity to a class of events or individuals. Use of the representativeness heuristic sometimes reflects a failure to take account of relevant "base" information given before a judgment has to be made, or a statistically invalid reliance on small samples (the so-called "law of small numbers"). In an early experiment, participants who were asked to guess the professional affiliation of a group of individuals who were brought before them, one after another. Despite being informed in advance of the percentages of the various professions within the group to be evaluated, the experiment participants greatly overestimated the number who were judged to be librarians, influenced as they were by characteristics that they associated with (that were considered representative of) librarians.

Failure to allow for "regression to the mean" (a reversion of individual results towards computed averages) was revealed in a study showing that most observers believed mistakenly about the "hot hand" in basketball (Continued belief in the "hot hand" surfaced in the NCAA March Madness of 2006 and was severely tested as the virtually unrated George Mason University basketball team defeated several presumably better teams, finally losing though in the semi-finals as the team's shooting average declined, reverting towards the team's season mean). Other experiments have shown that representativeness often lies behind much reasoning by analogy. Use of the representativeness heuristic, and others as well, tends to lead to unwarranted overconfidence, though overconfidence is a general phenomenon that seems to present itself even in assumptions about data such as one's knowledge of the basic facts that form a part of the decision problem.[5] (Overconfidence can be attributable to an illusion of control. Note also that studies have shown that overconfidence occurs more frequently with males than females.) Errors

---

[5] Overconfidence seems to be a common phenomenon (though less confidence than is warranted also occurs in some contexts, especially with some individuals). Both overconfidence and underconfidence can lead to decisons that are less than fully rational. Nonetheless, in this, as in other cases, behavioral economics needs to be more careful about characterizing biases of human behavior. More than casual empiricism is required, as a rule. Juan Dubra and Jean-Pierre Benoit have shown that the claims and alleged proofs of overconfidence that have been published to date are not adequately supported, and in many cases, are simply incorrect. Note though, that an alternative to a proof of overconfidence (or lack thereof) may emerge with the explanations of open-ended, in-depth interview based studies (which are discussed further in Section 9).

also can be due to a *lack* of confidence. Yet another problem is error in recall, which forms a part of many heuristics. A bias associated with much reasoning that does not involve complete calculation is a bias in favor of the status quo.

Psychologists and economists also have been taking note of other general heuristics, perhaps the most notable of which is loss aversion, cited originally as an anomaly in revealing the changing attitudes toward risk according to whether gains or losses are involved. Loss aversion refers to the tendency of individuals to value strikingly negative *outcomes* (such as bankruptcy) more than expected values which reflect the *probability* of those outcomes. (Ambiguity aversion, the tendency to avoid choices with ambiguous as compared to just simply unknown information, also comes to mind, though more as a bias in interpreting options. Ambiguity aversion can be thought of essentially as uncertainty aversion.) Another general heuristic, though one with mixed empirical support, is the use of regret theory, which involves contrafactual and introspective thinking, and employs strategies to avoid the intense negative emotions that can arise from imagining a situation that would have been better had one decided differently. Some analysts consider approaches to deal with cognitive dissonance (when an individual has conflicting preferences) as another general heuristic. Others refer to what is called melioration, an effort to replicate average rather than marginal results, which has been observed primarily in experiments with animals—but which also appears to affect the pricing decisions of some of the most sophisticated members of our society, physicians. Finally, most psychologists have come to regard affect as a leading heuristic (see Section 10).

Heuristics, short cuts to the search for solutions, generally involve biases, and biases which usually differ from one another. Solution of many problems requires more than a single heuristic, and, indeed, *specific* heuristics that take account of the type of decision making involved (sometimes referred to as the region of rationality), the particular context, and the likely significance of missing information. Beyond that, and perhaps most importantly, while data on heuristics and their biases should be recorded to be sure that they are adequately taken into account, and also so that there will be a stronger basis for developing better heuristics that will foster an improved decision making process (whether or not one tending towards optimization), in fact, decision makers rarely record the data on heuristics and biases. Some problems are so complex that they may not be solved reasonably efficiently by heuristics in the time available, but only by a kind of expertise that has been referred to as pattern recognition. That seems to be the way in which Grand Masters function in chess, and their situations involve options that are not nearly as complex as the changes in expectations and uncertainty often confronting leaders in business or public life.

Another aspect that can bias the processing of information has already been noted: the way in which information is framed, with particularly strong differences, for example, according to whether the information is framed in a positive or negative manner. (This has long been recognized by trial lawyers and those in marketing.) Dubious recall of information and the imperfect nature of information feedback can influence the evaluation of judgments and the use of the same approach in the future. Hindsight bias is important, but other factors enter as well, such as the reliability of the feedback, erroneous recall of reasoning processes, and misunderstanding of chance fluctuations such as the "gamblers fallacy," in which observers raise their expectation for the appearance of "heads" after a succession of coin flips resulting in "tails," even though the probability for an individual flip of the coin remains unchanged at 50-50.

What is termed intuition, also can be regarded as a heuristic. That imprecise phenomenon refers to a mix of analytical and affective reactions (including visceral factors, discussed in Section 10) that reflect subconscious as well as conscious aspects. A discussion of intuition can be found in Chapter 3 of Altman's *Handbook of Contemporary Behavioral Economics* by Roger Frantz.

The frequently high cost (and often impossibility) of undertaking optimizing calculations leads to a general use of decision making short cuts—heuristics. Some heuristics are of a general character but most are specific to the contexts involved. Almost all heuristics involve biases, which should be taken into account in making decisions, and awareness of which may enable improvement of the heuristics. As critical as work in this area is to behavioral economics, lack of a satisfactory theory of heuristics hampers any generalizable analyses. Some advances in our understanding have been made, however. A prominent example has been recognition that loss aversion, originally concluded to be an anomaly, is now regarded as a heuristic applying to a wide variety of contexts.

8

Intertemporal Decision Making and Procrastination

Benefits not available until a future date are less valuable than the same amount, available immediately. This is not only because existing assets have a potential for earning something during the periods ahead, but because the benefits in times ahead may not materialize, indeed, that the asset might not even survive. For more than half a century, there has been an almost universal tendency to discount future benefits exponentially—at a constant rate for each period. Economists have been doing this without qualification although Samuelson, who proposed this in the 1930s and Koopmans, who reaffirmed the approach in the late 1950s, both indicated their concerns with the assumptions of the approach.

In the real world people value many benefits differently in different time periods, and there are plausible arguments for valuing certain benefits more in a future time period than if they were discounted exponentially. To begin with, one's time preference may vary from one year to another, and that may be accentuated by changes in expectations. This is apart from any general consideration of how much one should discount costs and benefits at any point in time because they take place in the future. Moreover, as one observer has put it, there may be a conflict between what we plan to do in the future and what we actually do when the future becomes the present.

The variance in an individual's time preference may differ for different categories of goods and services due to factors such as the utilitarian or luxury nature of goods, and, in the case of investments, their relative liquidity. Some of the variance in time preference may have existed from the outset (such as our general desire for a sequence of incomes that improves over time over one that does not do so, but yields a greater expected value over the course of time), but most of the variance probably reflects shifts in taste (and in attitudes toward risk taking) given experience, changes in context and changes in expectations. There also may be a change in the inclination to take on debt due to a variety of cultural factors, temporary shocks to the economy, and, as marketers have learned, the way in which the matter is framed.

Numerous examples and an increasing number of studies have shown that much human behavior corresponds to such patterns. Time preference is in part a reflection of individual tolerance for patience, and also reflects the willingness to take defined risks (and to take on uncertainty, which cannot be readily defined), all of which may shift over time, influenced by changes in context, expectations and other factors. Time preference has been shown to vary with intelligence—with high IQ individuals likely to be more patient than those with lower IQs—though there are qualifications to this. Also, there are gender differences, with greater intelligence tending to make women more patient and men more inclined to increase risks and take on added uncertainty. Time preferences are not always consistent, however. That may be explained in part by the (varying) influence of emotional (and visceral) factors. (See Section 10.)

More generally, a preference for the future benefits of one object over another in the relatively distant future sometimes shifts as the dates of the two come closer to realization or as the second object is brought into closer view—i. e., the discount rates implicit in the decisions of people can vary, increasing as the time before payoff grows shorter, which reflects an increasing importance of time preference as the time horizon shrinks (or comes into sight). Discount rates also appear to vary for most people for different types of activity. In addition, though less uniformly, the interest rates implicit in choices between time periods change as the amounts involved become larger, with most people willing to accept a smaller rate of return for a delay in receiving $1,000 than $10 or $100. These are the result of empirical studies, not calculations of what is best, but they are factors to take into account when dealing in the real world and they may reflect something more than emotional preferences though they clearly reflect those to an important degree.

Some behavioral economists have shown that there are alternative systems that explain choices over time better than the exponential discounting approach that   mainstream economics and business administration would have us believe is the correct way to proceed, such as discounting that reflects a hyperbola (a hyperbolic discounting function). With hyperbolic discounting, we tend to choose a larger, later reward over a smaller, somewhat earlier one when both occur with a substantial delay, but switch to the smaller, earlier reward when the delay falls below some threshold. In the short run, the rate at which emotional and even cognitive factors may lead us to discount benefits may be quite high. That approach can alter the evaluation of projects; it may be viewed in large measure as a myopic result of emotional factors (in contrast with the calculation of the far-sighted planner).

Hyperbolic or quasi-hyperbolic models have been used in explaining real world growth, self regulation, information acquisition, job search, retirement choices, procrastination, addiction, and investment in human capital. The research on hyperbolic discounting suggests that changes in financial markets may influence welfare by altering the liquidity of assets, and, as a result, the tendency to consume. Although hyperbolic and quasi-hyperbolic discounting models appear to explain much real economic behavior better than the traditional exponential models, even those may reflect only a first approximation to what transpires; it is not clear that the hyperbolic variations best reflect human behavior in a variety of situations. Moreover, like the exponential discounting it would replace, the hyperbolic models that have been advanced also assume maximization of a utility function with a specific structure and thus miss much of the most important contribution of the psychological decision making process and behavioral economics, which shows that frequently maximization is not the objective, and, at any rate, is not fully attainable, as decision makers come to realize, however much they may use the word, optimization. Alternative valuations of benefits over time—which may lead to conflicts with the mainstream economic tenet of transitivity—seem to have most relevance to consumer behavior, especially to the presumably irrational tendency towards procrastination. Some business and investment decision making calls for discounting that is not the same in all periods as well; while procrastination is most common at the level of individuals, it also takes place in the marketplace, as the slow reaction of companies like General Motors and Ford to change despite the obvious wisdom of doing so makes clear.

People undertake many measures to influence intertemporal decision making and accept an increased role of outside control, such as that of government, especially with respect to saving and investment. Most of these involve self control pre-commitment, and are aimed primarily at overcoming emotional factors that explain low levels of saving and a disinclination to ferret out better investment alternatives.

While, as a general rule, it makes sense to value future benefits less than the same quantity of benefits available at some given point in time, the question is just how much less the valuation should be—how we should go about discounting benefits that are not available until the future. This is not nearly as settled as economists have been inclined to assume, either in an optimizing sense, or as a description of how people actually behave. The argument for traditional exponential discounting seems weaker than that for hyperbolic discounting as a description of how people actually behave, and even the latter may not most accurately reflect how people behave in some situations. While the objective of behavioral economics is not to determine what is most nearly rational in terms of mainstream analysis, in fact, in many situations the emerging approach of behavioral analysis may be more rational—more nearly optimizing—than the traditional exponential approach to discounting.

9

Empirical Techniques

Most data that economists use in their analyses come from observed (revealed) results and, less frequently, as in some surveys, from declared values. This has led to empirical techniques involving statistical analyses, laboratory experiments, simulations, and some case studies. Of these, laboratory experiments have been most emphasized.

Laboratory experiments began decades ago as an effort to test components of microeconomic theory. In the process the experiments have revealed many results that are anomalous with traditional economic theory. The laboratory experiments of economists have differed from those of psychologists, primarily in that the economists have insisted that participants be given significant incentives. The importance of incentives appears to vary with the nature of the task asked of participants and the importance of non-monetary considerations. Initially, most experiments tried to steer clear of context, though this is changing as many experimental economists now attempt to influence economic policy. The problems that have been addressed have been relatively simple, framed in a manner that is easy to understand, and have allowed the participants to make clear decisions, with time allowed for trial and error. Many experiments have allowed each of the participants to take, alternatively, all of the positions in a given laboratory experiment. Deception has been avoided, but generally, efforts have been made to capture the psychological process of actual decision making. The participants, overwhelmingly first and second year college students, have been relatively homogeneous, though this has begun to change somewhat as experiments have been conducted in more countries and with participants from a wider variety of educational or cultural backgrounds. The experiments have attempted to assure that the independent variables have been the sole (or at least the principal) source of the dependent action. The strongest aspect of laboratory experiments is the control that they offer, which is not possible in the real world.

Most who conduct laboratory experiments attempt to avoid reference to context, yet context is often critical to behavior in real life, particularly in complex situations. Moreover, emotions such as anxiety and stress appear to alter probability processing and performance more in the real world than in the laboratory (as do a variety of emotional factors for certain types of the decisions of different age groups—recall the reference to the social decisions of teenagers noted in Section 6, e. g.). Experiments may be influenced unintentionally by the beliefs of those who conduct them and, even more, by any (especially undetected) rules of thumb that participants in the experiments bring with them, as well as by a *lack* of the kind of heuristics that would come from having had certain types of real life decision making experience—probably common among the overwhelmingly student participants in such experiments. Indeed, the results also may be biased to the extent that the participants have preferences that are more homogeneous than the population in general, which is probably true of the student participants from the relatively selective colleges in most of the experimental exercises. The lack of deception in most laboratory experiments may sound admirable, but consider that deception is characteristic of a good deal of decision making in real life.

Field experiments overcome some of the limitations of the laboratories, but they have their own limitations. However, even field experiments indicate that individuals accept less uncertainty in real life than in the lab; there is more concern with survival than the maximization of outcomes (or high performance) in real life. In addition, in field experiments, the accumulated resources of real life decision makers may sometimes lead to results that differ from laboratory results in which there are no such accumulations, or they are assumed not to affect outcomes.

While many results of experimental economics appear to have wide application and have been critical to the development and reach of behavioral economics, some seem to contradict experience and what other types of analyses would lead us to believe. Additional limitations of experimental economics are noted throughout this overview, especially in the section on anomalies. Experimental economics may indeed now go beyond testing theory and provide guidance for some categories of ordinary economic behavior and public policy, but there is a need to indicate more than has been done to date, the limitations and the areas of decision making for which that is not true. Fortunately, this has begun; a few experiments are underway that introduce assumptions characteristic of real world activity.

With the exception of Simon and a few others, economists have not attributed much importance to examining the actual processes of decision making—to the reasoning underlying decision making and the explanations of economic agents for what they have done; there is a tendency to consider such material as unreliable, too subjective and relatively unyielding to statistical analysis. Recently, however, a few revealing, in-depth, open-ended interview-based studies have caused some behavioral economists to reconsider. I have contributed to this approach (see Chapter 18 in Altman's *Handbook of Contemporary Behavioral Economics*), but by far the most important of these studies was undertaken by general equilibrium theorist, Truman Bewley, who has become increasingly uneasy with the assumptions that the models of mainstream analysis ask economists to work with. Taking the various in-depth, open-ended interview-based studies into account, there are a number of reasons for including such approaches to the toolkit of economic techniques.

First, studies allowing for open-ended responses can reveal the inadequacy of the assumptions in some of the models of economic theory—that they are manifestly poor indicators of the reasoning processes which underlie decision making, thus enabling us to do away with a wasteful use of resources in testing those theories.

Second, by focusing on reasoning processes in real life contexts, the in-depth interview-based studies may help us develop hypotheses of how to implement more successfully, the recommendations that accompany good analyses. Implementation is an aspect to which economists have devoted little attention.

Third, while it is true that many interview-based studies may be necessary to provide a firm foundation for new hypotheses about economic behavior, even isolated efforts may uncover explanations that economists have overlooked, leading to the formulation of better hypotheses about economic behavior. These may derive directly from the interview responses, or those responses may stimulate researchers to construct new hypotheses. Moreover, case studies including in-depth interviews that reflect an improved understanding of decision making have been shown to motivate more successful behavior among those to whom the studies are disseminated.

Fourth, open-ended interview-based studies may help improve our understanding of the behavior that inhibits successful decision making, and better enable us to modify that behavior.

Fifth, in-depth interview-based studies may enable us to understand how better to take into account the biases almost invariably associated with the use of heuristics, how to adapt heuristics to different contexts and to changes in expectations, and, more generally, how to improve performance when lack of time, lack of data, the uncertain direction of technological change, or other dynamic factors simply prevent recognition of what would be best, not to mention calculation of what would be best.

One prominent behavioral economist maintains that open-ended interview-based studies are fruitful only when they deal with individuals who have good intuitions of why they behave as they do, but I doubt that such a limitation holds.

Behavioral economics is empirically based and has used a variety of techniques, with laboratory experiments occupying an important place, particularly in the early stages of developing the field. Less employed, but with much now to recommend them, are open-ended, interview-based studies. Bewley has shown, for example, that available economic theories do not explain downward wage rigidity in recession, while the reasoning revealed in open-ended interviews appear to go a long way towards doing so. Bewley's study of wage rigidity was based on more than 300 interviews, and his current analysis of price formation has involved approximately 600 interviews.

10

Emotion, Affect and Social Psychology

Some economists, experts in many other disciplines, and most in the general public have long criticized the assumption of so many economists that rational decision making is solely a *cognitive* process. Even with the breakthroughs in economic analysis provided by behavioral decision psychologists, the revised analysis of decision making set forth by behavioral economists remained overwhelmingly cognitive at first. The possible role of emotions was acknowledged, but almost always as something that *interfered* with rational decision making.

Several factors began to change that. First, it was shown that the role of different heuristics in triggering preference reversal is consistent with different emotions leading to different responses to key concepts employed in alternative presentations. This is the case in the preference reversal example of Section 6, which refers to the *probability* of an option, on the one hand, and the *price* that reflects the value of that option, on the other. Second, it was recognized that other areas of psychology such as social psychology also influence decision making.[6] This was shown initially for the field of finance, and it emerges even more forcefully in the insightful agendas for the incorporation of behavioral economics in health economics and the economics of organizations, as outlined by Richard Frank and by Camerer and Malmendier in the recent volume edited by Diamond and Vartianinen. Some note has been taken of the possible role of cognitive dissonance in influencing economic behavior, beginning with the work of Akerlof and Dickens, and, more frequently of such factors as herding instincts and groupthink (which assume that others know something that indeed they may not), the social influence of peer pressure and social emulation, social learning, the response to "momentum" trading and several communication phenomena, the latter perhaps best exemplified in Shiller's *Irrational Exuberance*. It has become recognized, moreover, that emotional factors sometimes *stimulate* us to undertake cognitive analysis in our decision making—though emotional factors also can contribute to

---

[6] Some behavioral economists emphasize the role of evolutionary psychology as well.

43

less rational decisions, decisions that are less in the long term interest of the decision maker, as has been often emphasized. Finally, Loewenstein has written on the role of *visceral* factors in decision making. Some of these underlie or contribute to what are generally considered as emotional factors, but visceral factors precede more complex emotional factors that also may involve cognitive elements.

In the mid-1950s Katona suggested briefly that psychoanalytic as well as psychological factors need to be considered in explaining economic behavior. There has been work in what is termed psychoanalytic object relations theory on personality development but few economists have endorsed this approach—although the behavior of certain prominent executives might seem to provide apt examples of its significance. After more than 300 open-ended interviews with business leaders and others to see if the leaders reasoned along the lines of major economic theories in their decisions not to lower wages during the U.S. recession of 1990-91, Bewley concluded that concerns about employee morale provided a better explanation than most of the other theories put forth by economists (and his explanation of the role of morale differed in an important way from that of a few others who also had attributed importance to the factor). Bewley explained convincingly that this was so and then speculated that the importance of morale was due in particular to the role of the unconscious.

The recent focus on the role of the emotions on decision making comes primarily from other quarters, however—from economist Robert Frank, especially in his book, *Passions within Reason. The Strategic Role of the Emotion*, from political scientist Elster, from economist/psychologist Loewenstein, and from psychologist Slovic and his colleagues. The next section will summarize recent findings from the emerging discipline of neuroeconomics, which appear to underlie many of the visceral factors and emotions that influence economic behavior. Note, though, that most of those who have presented evidence indicating that emotional, visceral and cerebral (neural) factors influence decision making are not yet ready to specify the *precise* role that such factors have on decision making and the degree to which that role is influenced by (and/or can be overcome by) context and efforts to alter the context (including by increases in incentives). Nonetheless, one recent study concludes that some simple decisions are made by the brain seconds before we actually become conscious of the issues at stake.

Visceral factors such as hunger, pain, thirst, sexual drive and drowsiness differ from emotions in that they are not triggered by beliefs and, for the most part, are not directed at particular individuals or groups, though this is less true for visceral factors such as fear. Deficiency in visceral factors decreases an individual's quality of life, chances of survival or likelihood of reproducing, as can be seen in evidence from the past. At present, these tendencies—and the need to take visceral factors into account in rational choice—are clearer for routine decisions than for more complex ones such as most of the most leading decisions facing business or government. In any event, there are many cases of people overreacting, acting irrationally against their own long term self-interest, and being completely "out of control" (though sometimes more or less aware of that). Most people do not fully appreciate the influence of visceral factors on current and future behavior and may exaggerate the importance of cognitive processes—although it is also true that some people may be too inclined, when asked how they made a decision, to respond, "by the seat of my pants," just to avoid difficult introspective analysis.

Visceral factors fluctuate and change more rapidly than tastes but they are temporary, correlated with certain circumstances, and thus, are usually predictable, particularly because they function with little or no conscious cognitive mediation. On the other hand, cognitive deliberation, often seen as a source of stability, can be a source of unpredictability. Visceral factors can produce a split between what one feels driven to do and what one feels it is best to do. Often people cannot recall accurately what visceral states felt like in the past and this leads them to misjudge, usually to underestimate their influence in the future; when people are strongly affected by visceral factors (when they are in a "hot" state and are acting impulsively) they have difficulty imagining themselves in a "cold" state and miscalculate the speed with which such a state will dissipate, leading to a bias in what they project for the future.

Strong visceral factors can influence people's immediate behavior more than they think is justified in normative terms, either beforehand or after those factors have dissipated, and because visceral factors are transient and generally not accurately recalled, people tend to underestimate the impact on their behavior. This is despite the sometimes important and long-lasting consequences that they have for themselves and for society.

Loewenstein notes several categories of viscerally affected behavior that are of special interest to economics: bargaining behavior, intertemporal choice, motivation and the exertion of effort, self-control and much decision making under risk and uncertainty. Visceral factors may help explain troubling simultaneous decisions to gamble and to purchase certain insurance (which, formerly, economists attempted to explain in solely cognitive terms), gender and age differences in risk taking, and sexually risky behavior. People employ a variety of strategies in an effort to manipulate their own visceral tendencies and those of others, beginning with the use of self-control mechanisms. Taking visceral factors into account seems to help explain some behavior that people view as irrational.

Until recently many assumed that visceral factors could be considered as part of emotion, but emotions involve cognitive considerations as well as physiological arousal, and are usually directed towards specific individuals, groups or institutions. Consider anger, hatred, guilt, pride, joy, anxiety, stress, grief, remorse, surprise, boredom, admiration, love, hope and frustration, but also counterfactual states such as regret. Some emotions are universal, while others seem to be specific to certain cultures. There is disagreement as to the degree to which emotions can be induced, the role of anticipated emotions, and the extent to which they can be controlled—on the effectiveness of strategies to avoid intensely negative and often counterproductive emotions, for example. Some examples of efforts to induce visceral and emotional reactions can be seen in advertisements for food products as "natural," cigarette ads which use that tactic as well as others to minimize the serious risks involved in smoking, ads with smiling faces, and the often influential background music of movies and television dramas. Emotions can improve decision making, in particular where natural choice theory is not able to resolve a situation and where no satisfactory rule of thumb is available, but they can also manipulate and undermine rationality, preventing us from thinking clearly about the consequences of actions. The impact of many motivations can be overcome (or reduced) by incentives, even by close monitoring. The interaction between emotions and material self-interest can best be seen in a cost-benefit model of emotions and in the economic analysis of regret. Expressions of guilt, shame, revenge, contempt, hatred and indignation are often counterproductive. The variety of emotions we have interact with each other to produce behavior, and emotions can shape preferences and choices in certain contexts.

Some recent work of psychologists focuses on motivation and mood (both of which are influenced by perceived ability), and on the multidimensionality of emotions as well as on cognition. Psychologists attempt to provide a conceptual framework for understanding the importance of emotions in guiding judgments and decisions, which they refer to as the affect heuristic. This is especially important in dealing expeditiously with personal attributes (in what is termed attribute substitution). Affective reactions to stimuli often occur first, automatically, subsequently orienting information processing and judgment. Some affect is present in all perceptions, but this appears to be truer for most everyday matters than for it is for much business and government data. The utility we experience may be colored by feelings of affect that have become associated with certain past events, and that may contrast with a parallel rational processing system involving decision theory. At the same time, it is doubtful that utility maximization (whether the maximization of profits or any other goals) is really what energizes human behavior in many circumstances. In any event, affect conditions our preferences, which may help explain why our preferences are not always stable even in the short run.

There is a strong relationship between images and decision making, ranging from predictions of preferences for investing in new companies to the predictions of the likelihood of adolescents to take part in health-threatening and health-enhancing behavior such as smoking and exercise. The precision of an affective impression makes a difference, as does the degree to which the decision involves a comparison. Proportions generally dominate actual numbers in guiding decisions, though if it comes to a matter of saving of lives, the option with the number of lives saved is regarded more than the one with the proportion saved. Warnings are more effective in vivid, affect-laden scenarios than when presented in relative frequencies. People are often insensitive to probability data when the consequences carry strong affective meaning, as with references to cancer, risks such as those involving nuclear hazards and toxic chemicals. Activities associated with cancer are seen as riskier and much more in need of public regulation than activities associated with less dreaded forms of illness, injury or death even if the overall adverse consequences of the latter also are quite high. In certain contexts (not yet well categorized), small probabilities can carry great weight, perhaps another and more important factor explaining the simultaneous election of gambling and insurance. Judgments of risk and benefit are negatively correlated and this does not change much with presentation of evidence to the contrary; the greater the perceived benefit, the lower the risk that is perceived. Some activities to which people react favorably are perceived as having low risk even when this is not true. The impact of the availability heuristic may be due not just to the ease of recall, but to recall involving images that bring affect to the forefront. Willingness to Pay for provision of a public good or a punitive damage award in a personal injury lawsuit may be influenced by emotional attitudes regarding those matters as by indicators of economic value.

Preliminary studies suggest that individuals with greater intelligence lean more towards cognitive rather than emotional solutions, but aside from problems sometimes caused by this, there are exceptions to it when powerful drives or emotions intervene. The tendency of greater intelligence to lead to cognitive approaches is influenced by individual experience and expertise, social, cultural and economic factors, but, unfortunately, the extent of these influences is not yet clear.

Although mainstream economics has considered rational decision making as solely a cognitive process, and the initial contributions from psychology's behavioral decision analysis tended to reinforce that, it is now clear that emotional and even visceral factors can play a role in improving the rationality of decision making—as well as in undermining it, as had been emphasized previously. Visceral factors are essentially physiological and evolve without thinking about them. Emotional factors (affect), are more complex, and usually involve cognitive thought. Ascertaining exactly how the various visceral and emotional factors influence decision making (and explaining the variations) remains very much a work still in progress.

11

Neuroeconomics

Neuroeconomics, a field initiated by the work of neurologists, explains the basis of at least some of the emotional and presumably all of the visceral factors in economic behavior. Eventually it may help explain all aspects of economic decision making, revealing how we are influenced by bio-regulatory signals to combine cognitive with affective and visceral processes. To do so in the most helpful manner, it will be necessary to be more specific about the precise role of neurological tendencies than is possible at present, and it will be necessary to indicate the degree to which those tendencies can be controlled or overcome in given contexts and with given incentives.[7] Although neuroscience was triggered initially by observations of humans with brain damage, economic decision making even of those who have been the most successful involves more automatic and emotional processing than we have been inclined to acknowledge. Neuroscience reveals the contributing roles of both automatic and deliberate or controlled processes and may be able to say something about decision making that reflects the kind of pattern recognition (pattern matching) referred to in Section 7.

The following attempts to summarize the most prominent view of neuroeconomics.

The brain is comprised of a group of systems and sub-systems that usually act consistently, but do not always do so. One group of brain mechanisms responds rapidly but in a relatively inflexible manner to visceral and emotional factors while other brain mechanisms respond to cognitive considerations, usually much more slowly. (Some cognitive brain functions are rapid, however, as in the case of visual perception.) The brain employs a multiplicity of systems to perform specific functions, though it appears that some functions are processed in different areas of the brain (costs are

---

[7] Several researchers have countered the contention of some neoclassical economists that much addiction to drugs can be explained as a rational calculation, for example, by showing that certain substances interfere with the normal operation of the neural system and inhibit learning.

processed in different areas than benefits, for example). This difference in processing areas is clearest for different types of thinking. Some responses of a visceral nature, and some of an emotional nature may foster, but others may conflict with cognitive reasoning. The existence of such quick, non-cognitive responses may be due to the contribution they make to human welfare, or that they contributed to our welfare at some stage of human development, as evolutionary psychology and other evolutionary theorists maintain.

Neuroscience is the study of the various components of the brain in undertakings including those involving complex decision making. Solutions are influenced by evolutionary considerations but also, in the words of one prominent neuroscientist, they "are heavily shaped by the specific circumstances and constraints...of the current...environment." Our cognitive facilities can be spectacular (witness the ability of Grand Masters in chess to defeat highly sophisticated computers in most trials, at least until recently, and of the best business leaders to outperform computers in even more complex business situations—perhaps best exemplified by the continuing successes of Warren Buffett, the world's richest individual, who claims that he does not even use a computer for his analyses), but, for most of us, our cognitive faculties are more limited. To begin with, most people can contemplate only one thought-provoking problem at a time, and may be severely constrained in the number of factors that they can consider simultaneously regarding that problem.

Neuroscientists have only begun to identify and distinguish the pathways of different types of responses to the same emotional stimulus, some of which involve only low-level sub-systems, while others engage higher level systems. Though it is clear that most—perhaps all—cognitive analysis responds to the affective system, we are not yet aware of the detail of many processes of affect. Neuroscientists need to understand better how particular emotions are engaged and interact with higher level cognitive processes and which emotional responses are likely to lead us astray, and, as Camerer, Loewenstein and Prelec have phrased it in their survey in *The Journal of Economic Literature*, for example, how environmental cues can trigger craving and increased demand.

At present, neuroscience tracks the activity of specific areas of the brain as various emotions are revealed and as cognitive tasks are performed.

Several types of scans are used, principally PET scanning (position emission tomography) and fMRI (functional magnetic resonance imaging). The second of these, which is currently being used by a number of economists, infers brain activity by indexing changes in local concentrations of blood oxygen which tracks the blood flow in the brain, using changes in magnetic properties due to blood oxygenation, this, in turn, reflecting inputs to neurons and their processing. It reveals correlations between brain activity and a task manipulation or behavioral response, but those correlations do not constitute a definitive estimation of causality.

Studies suggest that even in a point in time, some preferences depend on the particular conditions in which we find ourselves and the affective responses they trigger. Experiments with ultimatum games (see Section 12) have shown that offers that do not involve the would-be recipient in any costs but are regarded as unacceptably low, are rejected. That may reflect an optimal reaction in a world in which people interact with a small social group and there is a need to protect one's reputation over the long term (as may well have been even more markedly the case at some point in the past than at present). Moreover, we really do not know the degree to which the same responses would be repeated in real life situations. Indeed, one recent experiment indicates that people will exert extra effort to obtain profits or rents to the detriment of others in environments in which it is socially acceptable to do so; this would seem to limit the implications of the experiments on equity and fairness.

Some of the altruistic punishments revealed in trust experiments may be rational at a group level but may no longer be optimal in a highly structured society with other tests for enforcing fairness at a group level (such as taxes and regulatory controls). Other manifestations of altruism may have evolved over time in response to particular conditions. The different valuation of benefits in different time periods referred to in Section 8, may reflect different brain systems, different neural systems at work, at least in part; these may be influenced in turn by differences in the prevailing culture and environment and the culture and environment of one's upbringing, including any differences in the degree of self-control attributable to those factors, as well as to any differences in self control attributable to individual personalities. Note, too that we are sometimes motivated to take actions that do not bring any pleasure; there can be a disconnect between wanting and liking that is not taken into account in traditional demand analysis.

People react to calculable risk and incalculable uncertainty emotionally as well as cognitively—and there are often differences in results, depending on which dominates but it is clear from neurological studies that people understand the difference between risk, which is known in advance, and uncertainty, which is not. One study finds that much of the difference in the behavior toward risk in the case of gains and losses uncovered by Kahneman and Tversky can be explained in terms of the amount of neural activity required to select between sure gains and (larger) risky gains, on the one hand, and the only comparable mental effort involved in choosing between a sure loss and a risky one. Outlying cases such as the "gambler's binge" are still not adequately understood. Finally, consider that when we have the time, we often make cognitive judgments that conflict with those, perhaps more influenced by affect, which are made quickly, more influenced by the pressure of choice.

Neuroeconomics, with contributions from both neurologists and economists, explains some, and may help explain all of the factors involved in economic behavior. Indeed, some recent studies by neuroscientists conclude that the brain makes many simple decisions ten seconds before we become conscious of them. Neuroeconomics is based on analyses of brain mechanisms developed from fMRI and other medical machines—on correlations between brain activity and behavioral responses. The degree to which the tendencies revealed, even if causal, can be controlled or overcome has not yet been established. Several of the most prominent behavioral economists regard neuroeconomics as the most important element in understanding economic behavior.

12

Relative Considerations, Social Preferences, Justice and Happiness

Keeping-up-with-the-Joneses is a phenomenon that has long been recognized but economists have lagged behind those in marketing in attempting to take it into account. "Positional" goods were singled out by Hirsch, Frank and others, and have come to account for a significant part of demand. Cultural factors, what is socially acceptable and what is regarded as "fair," enter into preferences. This emerges most clearly from the results of the "ultimatum" and "dictator" games and the trust experiments (first introduced by the German economist, Güth). In an ultimatum game, one player is given a sum of money which that person, referred to as the proposer, is to divide with another individual, the responder, and is allowed to keep the proportion he proposes if the responder accepts the division. These games reveal that individuals will not accept money even with no strings attached and no labor or risk required on their part, if it represents a division of the proceeds which they regard as unfair. Such behavior is a departure from what economists have regarded as rational choice, according to which, individuals not required to make any effort or provide any expenditure, should be willing to accept whatever is offered. Moreover, the departure appears to hold irrespective of the financial condition of the responder—though that may not really have been tested adequately (and see, also, the qualifications just noted in Section 11). Nonetheless, procedural fairness is of some consequence; considerations of distributional and procedural justice matter—and the message seems to be that fair and moral behavior is required for success and perhaps even survival. There does seem to be an efficiency/fairness tradeoff, however, and independent of that, there is some resistance to uncompensated "free riding."

Along similar lines, the trust experiments show that individuals react differently to opportunities according to the trust they have of those with whom they are dealing (or according to the shared values they have with those with whom they are dealing), and according to the motivations that others have or that they believe others have. The last point can be particularly important because it allows for the importance of the perceptions that people have, independent of what reality may be, and this is a major threat to even an expanded interpretation of rationality. Also, most individuals react differently when they know how their choices will affect others.

The results in response to identical opportunities also differ according to whether the opportunities are presented as coming from an identifiable person or an impersonal outside force such as computer generated options—or an existing and transparent set of rules and obligations. Note that the degree to which there is agreement about shared values may be influenced by the way in which the questions about values are framed. Moreover, different emotions may affect different groups differently in their inclination to cooperate—even in the same society, not to mention, in different cultures.

Guilt appears to motivate cooperation in more cases than shame. Sanctioning systems can entail costs to those imposing them, and sanctioning systems for lack of response can yield better results than rewards for positive response. The laboratory experiments emphasize the importance of reciprocity in eliciting responses (reciprocal cooperation), and this appears to hold for options involving what economists have characterized as horizontal as well as vertical fairness. The message is that neither the self-centered maximizing extreme nor subordination of self-interest to a social group reflects the behavior that usually prevails in real life situations—though the extent to which behavior leans toward one extreme or the other does appear to be influenced by training and experience. The latter is especially true, for example, with respect to situations of continuing and increasing (or decreasing) private and social payoffs. The degree to which these results revealed in laboratory experiments reflect human behavior in real life situations is not yet clear—particularly in contexts involving major stress and adversity. The results would seem to contradict the tenet of opportunism that underlies mainstream economic theory as well as some popular assumptions. However, such responses may reflect primarily the continuance of responses to small group situations that were important for survival in early stages of human development, and which may not be as relevant for present day economic activity, as noted previously. Beyond that, behavioral economics must consider whether the laboratory findings (or which of those lab findings) are replicated outside the laboratory, as in the real life behavior of those who take part in the experiments, and, in particular, in business and other situations in which the contexts differ from (and involve much larger stakes than) those of the experiments. What Simon termed enlightened selfishness, which he found in the behavior of corporate subordinates, seems to be a real life approximation to the reciprocal cooperation identified in laboratory experiments. That behavior also would seem to reflect the potential role of group selection in explaining altruistic behavior.

Economists' studies of happiness reveal, as most people would have anticipated, that money isn't everything—that the happiness (or life satisfaction) that people report increases with income, but only up to a certain point, and that changes are attributable at least as much to shifts in one's position relative to others. While that is probably true,[8] the results do not yet seem to have been taken sufficiently into account, the fact that our memories of precise data (and feelings) have shown to be deficient. In addition, it is difficult to assess the extent to which happiness is related to income (even relative income) when, as is often the case, so many other matters are changing in the process. In any event, the happiness studies consider changes in "net" income without taking account of whether there have been any additional costs, not only in terms of money, but also due to factors such as leisure time lost, more disagreeable commuting, and added pollution in the society concomitant with the rise in "net income." The latter are aspects of what some have referred to as the self-defeating nature of happiness seeking.

Some goods and services appear to be chosen because of the position that possessing them is believed to give to those who have them, and relative incomes may be of more consequence than absolute levels in conclusions about welfare and happiness, at least above some basic level of income. What is considered to be the "fairness" of transactions and the motives presumed to be held, may determine the acceptance or rejection of offers—i. e., those factors may be basic to everyday economic activity. Factors such as guilt and shame explain some, perhaps much cooperation. Seemingly non-economic considerations may explain some economic decision making,

---

[8] One recent study casts doubt on these findings, insisting that absolute income does matter, independent of changes in relative income or the lack of them.

though it must be noted that such results are derived from laboratory experiments with real world verification still to be determined in many cases.

13

Opportunity Costs

In 2005 a study revealed that a large proportion of those who took courses in economics (and many of those who taught such courses) sometimes
identify opportunity costs incorrectly even though this concept, that of the
best option foregone, is one of the most fundamental concepts of economics. How, if at all, does the behavioral economics affect that finding?

Nobel Prize winner Coase maintained that goods and services not received are worth as much as the payments made for the same quantity of
the same goods and services that are received. This is a reaffirmation of
the principle that opportunity costs should be valued the same as equivalent out-of-pocket costs. Milton Friedman once stated that whether he was
a buyer or a seller of an item depended on the price; above a certain price
he would be a seller, and below that price, a buyer. Yet most people do not
believe that a gain foregone possesses as high a value as an expenditure
actually made or an out-of-pocket loss of the same amount, and the courts
have followed that approach in resolving disputes.

Further violations of the mainstream principle of opportunity costs are
suggested by a number of experiments. These have shown that when dealing with articles that individuals purchase which they do not intend to
resell in commercial transactions, there are large differences between the
value that they place on those articles (their willingness to accept or WTA),
and the value that most prospective buyers assign to those same articles
(the willingness of the latter to pay, or WTP). The differences have been
shown to be as much as 2 and 3 to1, and higher, even when participants
in the experiments were thoroughly familiar with the goods, and the items
used, such as ball point pens and coffee mugs, and were readily available
at local stores. The differences were much greater than could be explained
by any transactions costs or natural bargaining inclinations. This under-
mines the indifference curve analysis of traditional economics.

Repeated experiments narrow, but usually do not eliminate significant
differences. This "endowment" effect appears to occur as soon as one

comes into possession of an article, even a simple one—though perhaps it has been observed most vividly in the real economy with respect to more valued possessions such as homes, notably when they have not been purchased with quick resale in mind. This would seem to help explain the dramatic decline in the level of home sales in 2007, which preceeded the significant but slower decline of home prices in 2007-08. The virtually instant endowment effect is not a matter of discovering the qualities of an object, and, indeed, in the experiments, when sellers are suddenly placed in the position of buyers, they are not willing to pay the minimum price that they had just demanded as sellers. Moreover, contrary to what mainstream economics would predict, it makes a difference to the results, if the funds used for purchases are earned or obtained through some type of windfall.

What takes place in the case of sellers seems to be attributable principally to the pain of letting go of something—to the loss aversion mentioned in explaining risk seeking in the domain of losses by people who are risk averse when it comes to gains. Loss aversion seems to help explain why the level of transactions falls so much when the prices of real estate or stock shares decline. This disparity between WTA and WTP is important in considering the cost-benefit evaluation of public projects not subject to the market, for which it has been customary to assume that the more easily estimated WTP is the same as the much more difficult to evaluate WTA. Those who would lose scenic views or pristine streams, for example, tend to value them much more highly than the cost of the taxes needed to pay for the projects that would do away with what is there—or at least they claim that they value them more highly.

Even beyond such cases, cultural values can explain some choices that are inconsistent with opportunity costs as traditionally expounded, as in some of the trust games.

The concept of opportunity costs is loudly trumpeted as a basic consideration of economics, but it does not seem to characterize the way we often act. Perhaps that is why, as straightforward a concept as opportunity costs is, many students who take courses in economics and even some of their professors, have difficulty in identifying examples of opportunity costs when presented with seemingly plausible alternatives.

14

Applications

How much does all of this really matter to everyday decision making? How, if at all, does it alter what we would conclude by applying mainstream economic analysis?

Consider several areas.

A. Saving. Behavioral economists advising private corporations have shown two ways of increasing the rate of employee saving, recognition of which was incorporated into The Pension Protection Act of 2006 in the United States. First, make participation in an investment plan the default option, the one in which employees are automatically enrolled without having to make an active decision (allowing them to opt out later, if they wish to do so). When this is done, there is a dramatic increase in employee decisions to save, even in comparison with the changes that take place with options in which employees are not given the default option but are offered professional investment advice regarding the advantages of saving and investing more and then allowed to determine whether to participate or not. Second, when employees are asked if they will commit to an increase in their rate of savings out of any future increase in their salary, again, they end up saving significantly more than if they are asked if they would like to do so immediately after receiving a salary increase and are given investment advice and encouragement to save more (indeed, they save three to four times more).

The inclination to "Save More Tomorrow" means that individuals are willing to accept a lower discount rate for a given sum of money taken from future income than from current income. Such changes are important for societies in which the level of saving is low—or for any society in which increased savings and investment are sought. These options were suggested by behavioral economists, influenced by what the field has been uncovering. This shows that behavioral economics can achieve results not only by incorporating the findings about human behavior from psychology, the other social sciences and biology, but also by conducting its own experiments with respect to human behavior. To mention just one aspect that is not yet well determined, decisions to save—and to invest in certain instruments—appear to be affected by one's perception of household income as, in some sense, good or bad (adequate or not adequate for present and future purposes, taking all things including relative status into account). Unfortunately, no systematic mapping of the relevant behavioral factors is underway and the involvement of behavioral economists in practical matters has been rather limited to date, with the exception of the area of behavioral finance.

This may be on the verge of changing, however. See the numerous "libertarian paternalistic" suggestions of Thaler and Sunstein in *Nudge: Improving Decisions About Health, Wealth and Happiness*. Aimed at a general audience, the book shows how, given the lessons of behavioral economics, the basic principles of mainstream analysis, and considerations of public policy, well structured incentives from government and other institutions can get people to alter decisions (can nudge them) to make decisions that are more in their own interests than before. (The proposal to "Save More Tomorrow" was in fact a contribution of Thaler with co-author Benartzi.) Behavioral economists like Robert Frank would go further, and have government *require* some changes that behavioral economics has shown are preferred, at least in the aggregate, but that we seem reticent to undertake entirely on our own (or are not feasible on an individual basis). The more academic Diamond and Vartiainen volume, *Behavioral Economics and Its Applications* offers many suggestions on how behavioral economics could be incorporated into the fields of public economics, development economics, law and economics, labor economics, health economics, and the economics of organizations. The suggestions in the case of the last two are particularly detailed and promising. Much of the behavior of physicians appears to deviate from the traditional economic model of producer behavior. With respect to the economics of organizations, even the problems of arbitrage in correcting deviations from efficient market solutions noted by behavioral finance, significantly understates its limitations inside corporations.

B. Behavioral finance. An increasing number of those in finance have adopted the findings of behavioral economics to develop the field of behavioral finance. An important result has been to show that the Efficient Market Hypothesis, the hypothesis that the existence of markets assures that financial instruments are priced efficiently, does not always hold (certainly not in its extreme form), and, indeed, that the exceptions are numerous in the short-to-medium run. A growing number of investment advisers incorporate the findings of behavioral finance, and several investment funds now incorporate findings from the field, including one publicly traded group of funds which a prominent behavioral economics scholar helped initiate. The funds in that group include one characterized as "behavioral value," which has continued to experience 3, 5 and 10 year rates of return moderately higher than those of the leading stock market indexes.

Many studies have revealed that some financial phenomena can be understood best with models employing agents who are not fully rational in terms of mainstream financial and economic theory—agents who systematically act in ways that are counter to the potential for optimization where that is possible, who make what seem to be cognitive errors from which they do not seem to learn such as the miscalculation of and the failure to apply available information on probabilities, and who are obviously influenced by emotions and mood, beginning with such matters as sentiment-driven pricing of assets. One of the principal contributions of behavioral finance has been in explaining the limits of arbitrage, which does not succeed in correcting pricing errors (in eliminating discrepancies in market prices from fundamental values and from the prices in other markets) if traders who are not fully rational continue in the market for long periods of time (or others who trade on "noise" continue to enter the market), if financial institutions are reticent to lend prospective arbitrageurs large enough sums of money (or for long enough periods) or if they tend to call in their loans to arbitrageurs when the markets move against the latter, and if markets lack perfect substitutes for the incorrectly priced assets.

Among the aspects introduced into behavioral finance from psychology have been matters dealing with beliefs and preferences. The former include findings on framing, overconfidence and the illusion of knowledge, overoptimism, wishful thinking and the illusion of control, regret, and the heuristics, Representativeness, Anchoring and Adjustment, and Availability. With respect to preferences, psychology has had a strong impact through the introduction of Prospect Theory, through the analyses explaining choices when one or more options are unknown, and through the findings on ambiguity aversion.

Evidence supporting the significance of financial phenomena that are not consistent with models reflecting the tenets of mainstream economic theory include: the differing prices of the same stock shares—observed in the different prices for a number of years of the twin stocks, Shell and Royal Dutch on two leading stock exchanges; the much greater volatility of stock shares than the dividends on which the share values should be based; the apparently excessive premium of stocks to bonds (the equity premium puzzle); the ability to predict subsequent stock market performance of previous "losers" among stocks vis-à-vis "winners" (the lack of a "random walk"); the lag of markets in revaluing stock prices after earnings announcements that surprise; the persistence for some time of stock groups that earn rates above the market average; the apparent sensitivity of earnings to enterprise size; the continued reliance of some models based on beliefs but with insufficient allowance for institutional frictions; the findings of suboptimal excessive trading; the tendency of many investors to sell winners too soon and hold on to losers to long (the disposition effect); the long-time preference of dividends over capital gains; the increase in stock market activity—in the demand for stocks—when the prices of stocks rise; the lack of diversification or the naïve diversification of many investors; reasoning involving separate mental accounts when all involve the same fungible money; the different attitudes toward tax evasion according to whether income was earned or not; and the strong (though recently reduced) bias toward investments in national rather than global markets. Another probable indicator of the lack of solely financial considerations is the lack of any statistical relationship between factors such as the ratio between the prices and earnings of comparable groups of stocks. A caution concerning any mechanistic applications, however. In one recent experiment, prospect theory did not prove to be a good predictor of individual willingness to pay for investment products.

At this point, finance texts are being revised, and behavioral finance is growing in influence in financial markets. Its influence seems particularly great when it comes to what Zeckhauser has termed the unknown and the unknowable. (He maintains that extraordinarily successful investors like Warren Buffett, often cited as a traditional value investor, follow some important lines of behavioral reasoning): The financial crisis of 2008 should provide further impetus for the inclusion of psychological factors in financial analysis.

C. Marketing and Organizational Behavior. Marketing employs techniques that are consistent with some of the findings of behavioral economics, and Organizational Behavior stands out as a field in which several leaders have incorporated many of the results, as well as contributing to the empirical findings. This is especially apparent in the studies of Max Bazerman.

There have been fewer efforts to apply the findings of behavioral economics to many sub-fields of economics, however. The following considers the potential in half a dozen areas—labor economics, cost-benefit analysis, industrial organization, law and economics, tax analysis, monetary policy, macroeconomic analysis generally, and development economics.

D. Labor economics. For many years the analyses of labor have paid attention to empirical findings, particularly those from sociology. Those economic analyses stress the importance of fundamental sociological and cultural foundations of labor supply decisions. However, the incorporation of the new, more psychology-influenced behavioral economics has been slow, according to a recent survey by Berg in Altman's *Handbook of Contemporary Behavioral Economics*. In part, this is because even neo-classically oriented economists have long attempted to take more account of empirical realities than in many other areas. Nonetheless, few studies have incorporated the recent breakthroughs from cognitive psychology and few have been based on considerations other than narrowly defined self-interest maximization and fixed preferences.

Several recent efforts have considered the impact of relative wages and physical exhaustion in affecting effort, and have attempted to explain effort variability as attributable to relative wages, working conditions and the level of esteem felt by workers. Efficiency wage theories have been advanced (in explaining wage rigidity, for example), and, in turn, have been criticized by observations that employee shirking is often tolerated by employers. Conclusions about workplace morale and the psychological effects of unemployment have been gaining force, especially as a consequence of the in-depth interview-based study of Bewley. Psychometric measures of the mental states of workers have been introduced. This has been undertaken for groups that were unemployed or feared job loss, with efforts made to take account of the effects of the resulting depression on the brain's memory that may have been great enough even to offset subsequent re-employment and higher wages, which may have led to lower levels of productivity for those who experienced the unemployment.

More attention has been given to the relative position of workers and to "positional goods" as a part of increased attention to emotional considerations. Similarly, there has been a greater focus on the effects of stress, anxiety and extra effort on the work force. The variability of effort has been central to the analyses of x-efficiency, the less-than-optimal employment to which even efficiently allocated resources are often put. Labor analyses have emphasized the role of different production systems, of bargaining, of trust and of worker morale and of what are regarded as excess managerial pay on productivity, often independent of any explicit incorporation of findings from the other social sciences. A limited amount of attention has been given to loss aversion behavior in affecting labor supply, but more, to the effects of macro level cultural trends and possible preference changes over time.

The analyses explaining wage premiums for risky jobs is regarded as too dependent on numerous assumptions to invite generalization. The lack of satisfactory generalizations on the effect of taxes on labor supply also is unresolved for the same reason. Worker heterogeneity studies lead to conclusions that preferences are shaped by the environment, that the greater availability of high level employment affects fertility, the likelihood of women to remain married and the effect of marriage affects the productivity of spouses. Other studies have introduced cultural variables to help explain absenteeism, unions and the role of the work force. One of the most interesting efforts underway deals with the behavior of wages in the context of an interplay of presumably rational and boundedly rational firms. An area that has not yet been much explored is that of gender issues; Nancy Folbre has noted, for example, that while women have substantially increased their hours of market employment, men have increased their hours of non-market work much less so.

E. Cost-benefit analysis. When there is generally no functioning market for a good or service, as for projects dealing with dams and most so-called public goods, economists tend to make use of what is referred to as contingent evaluation analyses. This assumes that estimates of the willingness to pay (WTP) are a satisfactory proxy for often more difficult to determine, willingness to accept (WTA), consistent with the tenet on opportunity costs mentioned above and restated in the Coase Theorem, also referred to earlier. Yet the studies on WTP and WTA summarized in Section 13 showed that the two are often far apart. It is necessary to estimate both in order to arrive at a compromise estimate. In both cases it is necessary to pay particular attention to the framing of the questions (an aspect that the best contingent evaluation analysts were attempting even before the extraordinary magnitude of the differences to different ways of phrasing matters was documented by behavioral economists). Moreover, it is also of consequence to consider the magnitude of any endowment effect—and, the fact that some choices involve one or more goods or services that are not familiar to those making the selections, and thus, for which meaningful preferences are developed only after the choices have been made.

Another concern for all cost-benefit evaluations is the discount rate that should be used for projects involving costs and benefits over more than one period of time. The usefulness of many projects varies in different time periods, and for some individuals, the utility is greatest towards the end of the project (as in the case of retirement or bequest nest eggs), perhaps calling for hyperbolic, quasi-hyperbolic or another type of discounting that would alter the relative value of projects compared to that that which would be indicated by traditional exponential discounting. Both may greatly affect cost-benefit analyses, particularly the ranking of projects. Economists have joined psychologists in beginning to explore this area.

F. Industrial Organization. Few contributions from behavioral economics have been applied to industrial organization. Indeed, as recently as 2000, when asked why this was so, a prominent economist in the field replied (privately), "There's no demand for it." In Appendix A, a text in this area that does incorporate a few applications is critiqued, indicating where many additions might be made.

G. Law and Economics. The ties between economics and the law have been increasing. Even at present, though, U. S. courts have not been inclined to award damages for gains that were prevented from being realized in contrast with those regularly granted for damages actually incurred. They have not usually accepted the economic principle that opportunity costs should be valued as equal to out-of-pocket costs. Nonetheless, during the past two decades there has been a growing tendency to incorporate many of the principles of mainstream economics into the law. Basically, this has involved viewing individuals as having stable preferences, attempting to do the best they can, and possessing a level of information that permits optimization, or as possessing optimization objectives that lead to a search for the necessary information, either on their own or with the aid of advisors. The law and economics literature along those lines has been based on rational choice theory—that decision makers know the goals they seek to achieve and rationally pursue those goals. It assumes that they are cognitively capable of identifying the alternative means of goal achievement open to them and of evaluating the relative worth of the alternative means of reaching their ends. As rational decision makers, they have neither inconsistencies nor incoherencies in their preferences.

Unfortunately, that approach has involved, in the words of behaviorally oriented legal scholars, a failure to recognize the effects of bounded rationality, bounded will-power and bounded self-interest (a lack of the inclination to consider others, as in reciprocal cooperation). One of the most important consequences of these limitations is to deny the argument of Nobel Prize winner Coase that the initial assignment of entitlements will not affect the optimal ultimate allocation of resources so long as transactions costs and wealth effects are minimal; that position holds that any court adjudications in this area would often be modified by bargaining between the former litigants.

The initial distribution of property—the endowment—does matter in the way we actually behave, even if this is not rational in terms of the models of mainstream economic theory. One indication of this has been the intensity with which managers used to fight with labor to maintain prerogatives to which they had become accustomed, and the force with which labor unions have resisted surrendering privileges obtained over the years, even when survival of their firms (or industry) was at stake. Emotions certainly come into play. Further, notions of fairness rather than neutral considerations of efficiency explain much of what the legal system does (or endeavors to do), as can be seen in many of the laws that are aimed at helping the poor and disadvantaged, that place constraints on individual action. Beyond that, an increasing number of laws reflect real (or perceived) limits in the rationality or ability of individuals to protect themselves in their own interest. Sometimes that assumption is mistaken, admittedly, and in other cases, while those laws provide protection that is sought, they do so at costs that exceed the value of the protection provided.

Some prominent lawyers and economists are attempting to modify the movement to incorporate economic principles into the law so as to reflect the emerging findings of behavioral economics.

H. Tax incentive alternatives. Economic psychologists have long shown that the framing of tax forms and the accompanying instructions offered can lead to differences in the way in which information is perceived and the degree of tax compliance. Tax compliance also is powerfully influenced by social norms, individual ethics, the level of satisfaction with society, and the appropriateness of public policies along with the adequacy of the implementation of those policies. The appropriateness of policy refers to the efficiency of measures to achieve objectives, taking account of the cognitive limitations and the emotional factors noted in this presentation, the latter emphasizing especially matters related to horizontal and vertical equity.

The appropriateness and adequacy of the policies dealing with taxes depend in part on the degree to which enterprises—or any sectors of enterprises that are singled out—seek to maximize profits and are able to do so. Moreover, the general assumption that enterprises are risk averse, at least with respect to additional income, needs to be modified. Some enterprise leaders—particularly entrepreneurs in new activities—and some entire categories of industries, appear to be neutral with respect to risk and even a measure of uncertainty, and to be risk takers for a considerable range of income and profit. In addition, even risk averse enterprises, may be risk takers when losses seem likely, at least for initial amounts of loss—reflecting their loss aversion—(though several real world analyses suggest they are likely to revert to risk aversion at some point). Consider, too, that empirical studies have shown that other companies, particularly, long established large ones, may be risk averse, not only for situations in which losses are possible but even in contexts in which the expected value of overall outcomes are positive but there is some possibility of major adversity.

I. Monetary policy. The activities of the Federal Reserve System—interest rate regulations, etc.—relate primarily to monetary policy. As has been noted, money illusion is still very much with us. Most of us continue to fail to make entirely adequate allowance for inflation in dealing with changes in prices and there are differing perceptions even of recent rates of inflation. This is one factor, though perhaps not the most important in explaining inflation expectations. More important may be the tendency to gauge expected inflation by using the anchoring and adjustment heuristic—taking recent rates of inflation (or the perception of the recent rates for the various disaggregated components of the economy) and then adjusting them heuristically with some allowance for major visible shifts in current and expected tendencies in real factors in the economy. Other considerations in explaining inflation expectations are related to estimations of what an optimal rate of inflation would be, which in turn, is linked to issues such as those of price and wage stickiness and unemployment (including the so-called natural rate of unemployment). Note that the degree of money illusion may differ among various groups in the economy, and for different undertakings within the same group. The earlier work of the recently designated Nobel Prize winner, Edmund Phelps, seemed to invite the incorporation of some of the elements of behavioral economics that have been developed in the last two decades.

The choice of monetary policy instruments depends on the relative magnitude of the unexplained variability of the demand for money and the aggregate demand for goods and services, but these are based, in turn, on limited knowledge and include unpredictable changes in key macroeconomic relationships. The choice of monetary policy instruments, and the degree to which each should be changed ought to be based on the likely response of those affected by each of the instruments, in part a psychological consideration, and by exogenous factors, also, in part determined by psychological considerations. Behavioral economics adds doubts to the proposal that monetary policy should target the price level rather than the rate of inflation because so many behavioral determinants of the equilibrium price level remain insufficiently understood and apparently beyond the control of policy makers.

In addition to these and the considerations generally taken into account in mainstream economic analysis, the impact of monetary policy also is influenced by differences in the intertemporal discount rate employed by different groups in the economy—and the sometimes different rate that is used for different types of projects even by the same groups, by the degree to which there are switches between risk taking and risk averting with changes in the interest rate, and, returning to the first point, by the degree of money illusion.

Mere mention of these factors and our lack of understanding of them should throw light on the seeming inadequacy of recent monetary policy measures.

J. Macroeconomic analysis generally. A prominent European macro theorist remarked more than a decade ago that macroeconomic analysis dealing with the level of economic activity in the economy was in profound need of the types of considerations that behavioral economics was attempting to take into account. The promising potential is further suggested by the work of Thaler and others on saving, the advances in behavioral finance generally, and the contributions of Akerlof and Bewley in discovering better micro assumptions underlying macroeconomic behavior. The emerging findings on labor variability of Altman and others undermine mainstream models dealing with employment and productivity. Moreover, it is recognized now that models such as those based on rational expectations, with individuals and other economic agents behaving in a fully rational manner, neglect the costs of acquiring information, the asymmetry and faulty perception of the information available to economic agents in the same economic transactions, the recognition that economic agents may not seek to maximize (and, in any event, that they have a limited capability for doing so), the appreciation that tastes may not be fully formed and may not be stable, the fact that we lack a good understanding of what causes changes in expectations, and the fact that emotions are often very important. Unfortunately, there has been little progress in applying the behavioral approach to overall macroeconomic theory—few economists seem to be attempting to do so at present, even given the stimulus of the prevailing macroeconomic crisis. A final, if secondary note: in addition to the factors cited here and for monetary policy, consideration in developing a behavioral macro theory should be given to differences between the Willingness to Pay (WTP) and the Willingness to Accept (WTA) for the projects that are components of macroeconomic policy.

K. Development Economics. Few development economics publications reflect the findings of behavioral economics, even at the micro level where the case for application is strongest. Yet some laboratory experiments dealing with ultimatum games and trust experiments suggest that cultural differences sometimes explain differences in findings between countries (and between some ethnic groups within countries) with respect to what is regarded as fair. What makes the lack of these applications to development economics all the more remarkable is the conclusion of so many observers of trends in economic development that the failure to close the gap in income levels between the highest and lowest per capita income nations (and similarly, between the rich and the poor within nations) reflects a failure to achieve fairness in political and social terms. (Recently singled out, have been the concerns about the impact of globalization and ethical investment in the less developed countries.) Of course, the principal reason for including the findings of behavioral economics in Development Economics would be to contribute to a better understanding of the phenomenon of socio-economic development, incorporating new analyses of social and intangible capital to those summarized in this report, as factors helping to explain the potential for an increase in efficient growth as well as in social and political fairness. (As Mullainathan has speculated in the Diamond and Vartianinen volume, the phenomenon of loss aversion probably helps explain why changes are fought over so vigorously.) The revisionary work might begin with the inclusion of behavioral factors to explain some of the mysteries of international trade. An initial, but very limited effort to explain one of the most successful urban renewals of the 20th Century as reflecting the use of heuristics rather than calculation of what would have been optimal, can be found in this author's book, *Urban Renewal, Municipal Revitalization: The Case of Curitiba, Brazil* (Higher Education Publications, 2004).

15

Conclusion

Behavioral economics incorporates a long standing concern that the assumptions of mainstream economic models do not reflect most individual attitudes and commonly observed human behavior, with empirical work, most notably from experimental economics laboratories that has been spurred by findings in psychology, and now, neurology. Behavioral economics documents anomalies with mainstream economic analysis and reveals decision making that reflects not only cognitive, but also, emotional, visceral, and neural responses that are often different from the cognitive optimization assumed by most prevailing economic models, and that lead to better predictions.

The strength of recent behavioral economics lies in the scientific measurement and/or analytical rigor with which so many of those studies have being undertaken, the revelation of common behavioral patterns—and in the efforts to develop an underlying theory. Two weaknesses of behavioral economics are that the anomalies refer more to the short run than the long run, and that some (but not all) of the anomalies that have been detected are reduced once evidence of them is widely disseminated. Then, too, an approach that began with concern whether economic analysis was sufficiently realistic has been reticent to undertake empirical work that deals with the reasoning of consumers and producers in real world settings or that attempts to subject its laboratory participants to follow-up verification in the real world (the limited number of field studies in "natural surroundings" notwithstanding).

These factors may help explain why the impact of behavioral economics is still quite limited—though another reason is a concern that the cost of making many of the modifications in the analysis might not yield sufficiently offsetting benefits in enough cases. The most important reason for the lack of attention to behavioral economics probably is that there is still much to be gained by applying the imperfect tools at hand. The irony, nonetheless, is that behavioral economics is being applied least in areas such as macroeconomics and development economics, where, though the effort would be more difficult, the payoff might be greatest. Still, the inroads of behavioral economics have been noticeable, articles reflecting a behavioral orientation often appear in the leading journals, and the results of many of the studies are being disseminated in circles that until only recently, ignored the approach or heaped scorn upon it, with areas such as finance taking advantage of what has been found and turning it into cash dividends. Behavioral economics complicates economic analyses a good deal, but given economics' mediocre record of predicting, that is not necessarily a damaging observation.

In closing, consider several contributions that behavioral economics might offer to aid decision making with two major concerns of the day— global warming and health insurance.

Health insurance already is dealt with in a manner broader than that espoused by mainstream economics, with attention to how the programs should be altered. The analyses have dealt as well with how even the current, limited system should be made financially viable—how the costs of medical insurance should be paid for, how the costs might be reduced to levels more in line with other developed countries, and how the funds contributed to government (and private) programs should be invested. The first point usually is treated primarily as a matter of fairness and justice, but there is sometimes also note of the costs to a society of not providing all with coverage, particularly the young in the most formative stages of their life. The second also is dealt with in part in equity terms, though it is noted as well, that much of the problem of cost imbalances comes from increases in our life expectancy far beyond the age when benefits initially were planned to become available, and the continuing decline in the ratio of the system's contributors to beneficiaries.

Global warming is generally dealt with as a failure to take into account, the full costs of various activities, current ones, as well as many that have been with us since the onset of the Industrial Revolution. The discussion tends to deal with those costs and the alternatives that might replace or reduce them, namely the reduction of energy consumption, alternative fuel options, and pollution transfer allowances. Intergenerational equity issues also are noted, but those considerations are sometimes masked by disagreements over the extent of global warming that is likely, given current or little more extensive means to modify current activities.

The health insurance issues might be addressed, first by taking account of the way in which the problems are framed, which might lead, not so much to different diagnoses as to different recommendations for dealing with the problems. Second, there might be an effort to distinguish between the elements of risk, which are calculable, and those of uncertainty, which reflect unknown, often unknowable factors. With respect to the latter, it would be helpful to group the issues of uncertainty in several categories, according to whether the range of change in the data, while uncertain, is likely to be only moderate, whether the changes are likely to be very great, or whether the changes are simply unfathomable. To what extent do the limits of bounded rationality require the use of the type of heuristics discussed above, involving serious biases? Perhaps those limits are less pronounced than for some other areas of public and private decision making, and, if so, this should be noted. In taking account of strategic interaction, what can be said about still relatively heuristic type approaches—approaches other than behavioral game theory that are probably much more in use but have yet to be analyzed to any degree? How much difference do hyperbolic alternatives to the commonly used exponential discounting alter the diagnoses? Here, too, the answer may be less than for other areas of policy. Finally, there is need for a candid appraisal as to which recommendations (or the degree to which various recommendations) are influenced by emotional, not only cognitive factors, and the former, in turn, by issues of fairness—between different groups in the population, and, intergenerationally.

The global warming debate has centered on the probabilities that various phenomena will lead to different degrees of warming, the consequences that this will have for different locales, and the cost of alternative ways that further warming might be reversed or at least slowed down. The manner in which the (adverse) alternatives are framed can make a difference, but unlike the situation of medical insurance, framing considerations may not be where behavioral economics has its key role. A more important contribution would be to distinguish between groups of uncertainties, as suggested above (with its being possible to distinguish between some uncertain changes likely to be only moderate, others likely to be very great, and still others, simply unknowable). Some recognition might be given to whether the approach of individuals to uncertainty in this area is like that of their approach to earthquakes—ignoring low probabilities before they occur—or more like their reaction to gambling—overestimating the low probabilities and with less of a sense of loss aversion than in many other activities. This, as well as a tendency towards hyperbolic type discounting may be part of the explanation of what seems like procrastination.

Another factor is the fact that some of the consequences of projected alternatives are not well enough comprehended to enable clear preferences in approaches; although we do make some choices even without fully informed preferences, making choices when some of the alternatives are not well understood is not a basis for sound policy. Indeed, the latter may explain, better than the assertion of procrastination, many of the delays in selecting between alternative measures to alleviate the threat of global warming. Given the extent of the unknowns, emotional factors enter even more in relation to cognitive ones than for many other areas of choice. Considerations of fairness and justice may not be as apparent as in the case of health insurance, but those who could be singled out as likely to be major losers in the event of the adoption of measures to alleviate global warming probably would be more willing to take the impacts to others into account if major differences in the *relative* impact to different groups that are likely to result from global warming, could be clarified. It might even help if it could be shown that the estimates of projected losses as a consequence of certain measures to alleviate global warming are influenced a good deal by the particular way in which costs and benefits are discounted and that plausible alternative ways of discounting would change the findings.

The limits of full rationality undoubtedly are greater for global warming than for health insurance. Moreover, the heuristics are likely to be less developed and more biased, and the usefulness of pattern recognition, so important in many business situations, is likely to be particularly limited. Concern with the welfare of others might be promoted and possible compensation schemes devised if studies were to attempt to estimate the probable impacts of global warming on different groups, if those proved to differ greatly between groups. Similarly with intergenerational effects. It is urgent that we consider a wider range of strategic interaction alternatives. Finally, in dealing with both health insurance and global warming it will be necessary to grapple with the implications of alternative sets of expectations.

With these types of additions to the diagnoses and evaluations of these two areas, the introduction of concepts of behavioral economics may demonstrate its capability of helping to shape decision making in more—and increasingly major—areas of public policy.

Appendix

Industrial Organization (IO)

Major applications of IO have been made in recent years, involving not only antitrust, but also, the regulation of public utilities, public and private workplaces and the environment, and communications channels, virtually all using mainstream economic analysis, spurred by developments in Law and Economics, and spearheaded by Richard Posner, the distinguished jurist and professor of law. What follows provides a critique of the third edition of one of the few IO texts to introduce some of the findings of behavioral economics (though only in one section of the book). That text, the *Economics of Regulation and Antitrust* by W. Kip Viscusi, John M. Vernon and Joseph E. Harrington, has provided guidelines for many practitioners, particularly following Viscusi's teaching the subject matter for a number of years at Harvard and Vanderbilt Law Schools.

The *Economics of Regulation and Antitrust* slips back and forth in its assumptions between optimization (notably in dealing with competition and monopoly) and those of an almost satisficing nature (in dealing with much regulation of business). However, even with respect to the latter, it does not note that the attainment of objectives may be constrained by the cognitive limitations of individuals or by visceral and emotional factors. Moreover, while the text asks what regulators maximize, the question might better be, What objectives do regulators attempt to pursue?

Viscusi et al. does not provide guidance for decision makers in dealing with low probability, high consequence events such as flooding, tornados and earthquakes, or for the behavior of an important group of successful firms. Some studies show that the behavior of the latter tends to deviate from the profit maximizing inclinations generally assumed, particularly since maximizing behavior allows for a possibility of business failure, and many such firms take strong measures to thwart such a result.

The book discusses the Structure/Conduct/Performance paradigm that has often guided antitrust proceedings without introducing recent find-

76

ings from psychology and the other behavioral sciences to help establish ranges for which (or situations in which) certain conduct is likely (or unlikely), and for which it is likely to constitute more competitive (or less competitive) behavior.

Viscusi et al. acknowledge x-inefficiency, the less-than-fully efficient use of even well allocated resources, but attribute it solely to the lack of competitive pressure, ignoring the possible role of problems of perception and judgment. Moreover, the text ignores the fact that the different heuristics that are employed by decision makers may trigger different (and conflicting) responses, as in the case of the preference reversal studies, reflecting the different biases of alternative calculation short cuts.

Although Viscusi et al. note differences in the definition of barriers to entry, the book does not consider whether enterprises are impeded by the *perception* of the barriers in addition to the actual barriers themselves—which may lead to some differences in the conclusions. There is no consideration of the perception of markets and of competitive threats.

The text presents very summary comments on the importance of coordination, and at that, almost exclusively in the context of collusion agreements, ignoring material on the difficulties of coordination within firms, noted by many authors as a serious problem (to which Milgrom and Roberts have made important contributions). The discussion does not touch on the experiments of the past decade dealing with reciprocal coordination, or on what is perhaps the closest real world approximation of that, what Simon referred to as enlightened selfishness of subordinates in corporations, both of which can lead to major differences from analyses employing the traditional assumptions of maximization.

The exposition of game theory, which is used extensively in IO, does not incorporate the work of behavioral game theory. Game theory, a branch of applied mathematics, specifies the optimizing interaction between individuals—a behavior consistent with rationality in the terms of traditional economic analysis. Behavioral game theory modifies the assumptions about human behavior so as to be consistent with the findings of behavioral economics. It involves a broader definition of rationality, reflecting social norms that are required for the functioning of economic systems, and, in part, it reflects behavior, which, whether or not entirely rational in a broader sense, is repeated regularly and can be expected—such as a tendency to resort to focal points, the phenomena of overconfidence and that of loss aversion. Some of the results of behavioral game theory differ from those of traditional game theory, reflecting behavioral assumptions that are empirically based and sometimes differing from the universally optimizing assumptions of traditional economics. Game theory is applied mathematics, but the applied game theory that is applicable to industrial organization and to other areas of economics must be an empirically verified variation that takes account of psychological considerations. Beyond that, as has been noted above, it is necessary to take note of a wide range of strategic interaction alternatives, of which game theory (even behavioral game theory) is just one.

The treatment of dominant firm/fringe firm behavior does not consider how the use of bounded rationality heuristics and the problems of implementation might affect an analysis so dependent on assumptions of maximization.

The discussion of feedback relationships would benefit from consideration of less-than-fully rational but predictable responses, from what has been characterized as intuitive reasoning, from "horizon scanning," and from behavioral game theory.

The text deals with vertical integration as an optimizing means of reducing transactions costs but does not consider whether it may also serve as an insurance mechanism or as a heuristic to cope with situations in which optimizing seems overly difficult.

Viscusi et al. does not consider that some arrangements involving price discrimination may represent, not mechanisms to maximize, but the use of simplifying heuristics, and may not, in fact, lead to greater maximization.

The text deals with the pricing power of monopolists, but does not consider several aspects, among them behavioral ones such as when a firm gains monopoly or dominant status but does not raise prices because it misjudges important variables.

There is no consideration of the problems of implementation, the types of situations in which the problems of implementation are likely to be great, and whether this would alter the analysis.

Given the conflicting findings of the studies concerning the regulation of utility rates outlined in the text, it would be useful to have laboratory experiments and open-ended interview-based studies to see if they might contribute to the development of alternative analytical models. The book does not consider whether some adverse responses to deregulation reflects inadequate deregulation (reflecting a lack of a Just Noticeable Difference perhaps), or unrecognized behavioral responses (such as in inadequate regulatory fit, given motivations). The statement that economic efficiency may sometimes require pricing which conflicts with notions of fairness needs to be coupled with the findings of the ultimatum and trust experiments, with which they may be in conflict.

Several discussions would benefit from note of endowment effect studies that reveal major differences between Willingness to Pay and Willingness to Accept.

The discussion of franchising and auctions should take account of the fact that some Federal Communication Commission spectrum auction findings reveal that predictions derived from mainstream economic theory regarding the likely number of auction participants and the behavior to be expected from them, have proved highly inaccurate.

The text needs to consider the kinds of response that can be expected from particular types of regulation (and particular types of presentation) in the light of the use of heuristics, the findings of experimental economics and experimental psychology, and the earlier studies of economic psychologists (such as those dealing with differential tax compliance with different types of tax forms).

Viscusi et al. needs to consider the role of framing in influencing decision making in general, especially in the case of low probability, high consequence events (which may be particularly subject to distortions resulting from "availability cascades"), but also in a wide variety of aspects, among them, sensitivity analyses.

The discussions of environmental factors do not consider the role of emotional behavior. Moreover, the evaluation of enforcement and performance might attempt to take account of the role of, and motivating forces underlying corruption, though perhaps taking note of the seemingly less adverse effect of corruption on allocational efficiency and economic growth in some cultures than in others, at least in some contexts.

The nature of plausible behavioral responses should be considered in evaluating patents and alternative mechanisms to foster innovation.

Finally, the discussion of cost benefit analysis does not take account of the factors noted in Section 14E.

Bibliography

A.   A Few Introductory Readings on Behavioral Economics

Ariely, Dan. 2008. *Predictably Irrational. The Hidden Forces that Shape Our Decisions.* New York: Harper. A lively presentation of the ingenious experiments that Ariely and his colleagues have undertaken in the area of consumer behavior.

Bazerman, Max. 2005. *Judgment in Managerial Decision Making.* Sixth Edition. New York: John Wiley & Sons. Intended primarily for classes in Organizational Behavior. Contains a substantial bibliography, especially of articles written by psychologists.

Belsky, Gary and Thomas Gilovich. 1999. *Why Smart People Make Big Money Mistakes—and How to Correct Them. Lessons from the New Science of Behavioral Economics.* New York: Simon & Shuster. Quite basic, aimed at a general public.

Frank, Robert H. 2007. *The Economic Naturalist: In Search of Explanations for Everyday Enigmas.* New York: Basic Books.

Frank, Robert H. 1988. *Passions Within Reason. The Strategic Role of the Emotion.* New York: W. W. Norton. Aimed at a general public but more sophisticated than Belsky and Gilovich.

Schwartz, Hugh. 1998. *Rationality Gone Awry? Decision Making Inconsistent with Economic and Financial Theory.* Westport, CT and London: Praeger. The first chapter does not assume any knowledge of economics, the rest is aimed at those who have completed an introductory course in economics, particularly those taking microeconomic theory. Extensive bibliography, many items annotated.

Simon, Herbert A. 1986. "The Failure of Arm Chair Economics." *Challenge* Vol. 29, No. 5 (November-December): 18-25. Accessible to the general reader.

Thaler, Richard H. and Cass R. Sunstein. 2008. *Nudge. Improving Decisions About Health, Wealth and Happiness*. New Haven, CT: Yale University Press. An innovative integration of the experimental and anecdotal material of behavioral economics, basic principles of mainstream analysis, and ongoing public policy considerations, combined to build a strong "libertarian paternalistic" case for "nudging" changes in public but also private decision making.

B.   Selected Intermediate Level Material

Frank, Robert H. 2006. *Microeconomics and Behavior, 6th ed.*. New York: McGraw Hill.

Katona, George. 1975. *Psychological Economics*. Amsterdam: Elsevier. Especially useful on the evolution of the surveys of business and consumer expectations and plans.

Leibenstein, Harvey. 1976. *Beyond Economic Man. A New Foundation for Microeconomics*. Cambridge, MA: Harvard University Press. A full version of the x-efficiency thesis.

Shefrin, Hersh. 2000. *Beyond Greed and Fear. Understanding Behavioral Finance and the Psychology of Investing*. Boston: Harvard Business School Press. For the practitioner in finance.

Shefrin, Hersh. 2007. *Behavioral Corporate Finance. Decisions that Create Value*. Boston: McGraw Hill, Irwin. For MBA courses in corporate finance and behavioral finance.

Shiller, Robert J. 2005. *Irrational Exuberance.*2nd ed. Princeton, NJ: Princeton University Press. The first edition correctly forecast the stock market crash of 2000, and this edition correctly predicted the significant decline in housing.

Sunstein, Cass R., ed. 2000. *Behavioral Law & Economics.* Cambridge: Cambridge University Press.

Thaler, Richard H. 1992. *The Winner's Curse: Paradoxes and Anomalies of Economic Life.* New York: Free Press. Reprints of articles originally from the *Journal of Economic Perspectives.* (Others followed in subsequent years.)

C. <u>A Group of More Advanced Publications</u>

Altman, Morris, ed. 2006. *Handbook of Contemporary Behavioral Economics. Foundations and Developments.* Armonk, NY and London: M. E. Sharpe. A useful supplement to Camerer, Loewenstein and Rabin.

Bewley, Truman. 1999. *Why Wages Don't Fall During a Recession.* Cambridge, MA: Harvard University Press. The first major study based on open-ended, in-depth interviews.

_____. 2002. "Interviews as a Valid Empirical Tool in Economics." *Journal of Socio-Economics*, Vol. 31, No. 4: 343-53.

Camerer, Colin F., George Loewenstein and Matthew Rabin, eds. 2004. *Advances in Behavioral Economics.* Princeton, NJ and Oxford: Princeton University Press. A compilation of the leading theoretically oriented materials on behavioral economics.

Conlisk, John. 1996. "Why Bounded Rationality?' *Journal of Economic Literature*, Vol. 34, No. 2 (June): 669-700.

Diamond, Peter and Hannu Vartianinen eds.2007. *Behavioral Economics and Its Applications:* Princeton and Oxford: Princeton University Press.

Ekert-Jaffe, Olivia and Shoshana Grossbard, 2007. "Does Community Property Discourage Unpartnered Births." Paper presented to the 25th Anniversary Conference of the Society for the Advancement of Behavioral Economics, New York University, May 15-18, 2007.

Gigerenzer, Gerd and Reinhard Selten, eds. 2001. *Bounded Rationality: The Adaptive Toolbox*. Cambridge, MA: MIT Press. Heuristics as often efficient rather than essentially biased measures.

Gilovich, Thomas, Dale Griffen and Daniel Kahneman, eds. 2002. *Heuristics and Biases: The Psychology of Intuitive Judgment.* Cambridge: Cambridge University Press.

Gintis, Herbert, Samuel Bowles, Robert Boyd and Ernst Fehr, eds. 2005. *Moral Sentiments and Material Interests. The Foundations of Co-operation in Economic Life.* Cambridge, MA and London: MIT Press.

Kahneman, Daniel and Amos Tversky. 1979. "Prospect Theory: An Analysis of Decisions Under Risk." *Econometrica*, Vol. 47, No. 2 (March): 263-91. The key article of modern behavioral economics (written by two psychologists).

_____, Paul Slovic and Amos Tversky, eds. 1982. *Judgment under uncertainty: Heuristics and biases*. Cambridge: Cambridge University Press.

_____ and Amos Tversky, eds. 2000. *Choices, Values and Frames*. Cambridge: Cambridge University Press.

Maital, Shlomo, ed. 2007. *Recent Developments in Behavioral Economics*. Cheltenham, UK and Northampton, MA: Edward Elgar.

Simon, Herbert A. 1982, 1997. *Models of Bounded Rationality*. 3 vols. Cambridge, MA: MIT Press. (Leading contributions that provided the foundations of behavioral economics.)

Shleifer, Andrei. 2000. *Inefficient Markets. An Introduction to Behavioral Finance*. Oxford: Oxford University Press.

Slovic, Paul. 1995. "The Construction of Preferences." *American Psychologist*, Vol. 50,No. 5 (May): 364-71.

Thaler, Richard H., ed. 2005. *Advances in Behavioral Finance*. Vol. II. Princeton, NJ and Oxford: Russell Sage Foundation and Princeton University Press.

Wilkinson, Nick. 2008. *An Introduction to Behavioral Economics*. Houndmills, Basingstoke, Hampshire, UK and New York: Palgrave Macmillan.

Index